TOU[...]

B[...]

GREATNESS

DOROTHY KELLEY PATTERSON

"Behind every great man . . . are many influential women! Dorothy Patterson's newest book *Touched by Greatness* illustrates that truth through an insightful look at the women whom God used to mold Israel's greatest leader, Moses. Dr. Patterson does a masterful job painting a complete portrait of these women who have been only names on a page to most of us. The inductive study questions at the end of each chapter help the reader apply timeless biblical truths to everyday life. I enthusiastically recommend *Touched by Greatness* for both individuals and small groups looking for a fresh, applicable study from God's Word."

ROBERT JEFFRESS,
Pastor, First Baptist Church, Dallas, Texas

"*Touched By Greatness* is one of the best books/Bible studies on women I have ever read! Mrs. Patterson has taken a unique approach to looking at the lives and life lessons of women touched by God. I love the interesting facts, exegetical notes, and personal questions. It is thoroughly engaging, practically enriching, and extremely relevant for women today who have been and want to be touched by God."

DEBBIE STUART,
Director of Women's Ministry, Prestonwood Baptist Church, Plano, Texas

"Dorothy Patterson is a born Bible teacher, an extraordinary writer, and a marvelous mentor for Christian women everywhere. Her new book, *Touched By Greatness*, gives the reader a unique glimpse into the lives of Moses and the women that humanly helped enable his greatness in God's work. Throughout the book, Dorothy Patterson shares intimate stories in her own life, giving the book a deep richness. I highly recommend this book for Bible study teachers and group leaders, and for those readers who desire to know more about Moses and the women in his life."

DENISE GEORGE,
Author, Teacher, Speaker, Birmingham, Alabama

"*Touched by Greatness* is a wonderfully informative, amazingly creative, and ultimately practical and challenging book of encouragement for women to become all that God meant for them to be in His service. At the outset, Dr. Patterson challenges the reader by acknowledging Moses' disobedience toward God and the costly price that follows disobedience 'even for a great man.' Dr. Patterson notes how each of the women in Moses' life exhibited courage and extraordinary leadership for their time, and she discusses those factors that equip a woman, regardless of her giftedness or her position in life, to be used mightily by God.

"Each section of the book includes facts about the woman who is the focus of the chapter, along with parallel references, teaching notes, historical examples, quotes, a prayer and 'Dorothy's Dictums.' *Touched by Greatness* is a gripping story of ancient women that is brought to life by Dorothy

Patterson's keen insights. Every aspect of the women's lives is backed up by scriptural references and careful documentation for historical accuracy, but the ultimate impact of the book comes from Dr. Patterson's keen insights into human nature and thorough understanding and appreciation for God's grace. Dorothy's personal examples and stories add a human dimension to women who otherwise would be inspiring strangers. Instead, we see multi-dimensional women who are like us yet are still used by God to fulfill His purposes. In short, *Touched by Greatness* is a book that will inspire, challenge and encourage women to be more Christ-like in their everyday lives. This book will help women understand the importance of their unique and meaningful roles – even when the world does not take note or reward their efforts. Dr. Patterson's wisdom makes clear that whatever we do for Christ – whether in a major role or one in the background in service to others – will last and count for eternity."

JANICE SHAW CROUSE,
Director and Senior Fellow, The Beverly LaHaye Institute,
Concerned Women for America, Washington, D.C.

"Dr. Dorothy Patterson masterfully unveils a thorough analysis of historical women who were used mightily of God in the life of the great leader, Moses. This superbly rich and grippingly fascinating read presents the enormous impact and influence women can have on others as they passionately embrace the vision God has placed before them. *Touched by Greatness* will educate today's leader in a deeper understanding of extraordinary women often overlooked in the Old Testament as well as stir the soul with an overwhelming reminder of Yahweh God's providence. Dr. Dorothy Patterson presents deep biblical insights and unchanging principles pertinent to the 21st-century woman."

MONICA ROSE,
Professor of Women's Ministry, Liberty University, Lynchburg, Virginia

"Dorothy Patterson is one of the most engaging teachers I have ever had the privilege to sit under. As she writes this new book *Touched by Greatness*, she once again has captured the student's heart and mind with her approach to the women in the life of Moses. Not only does she teach the scriptural text, she includes history, quotations, illustrations, interesting facts surrounding the woman, and even a teaching outline to make it so practical for anyone to use this to teach others. This will be one book all women will want to read and then share!"

CHRIS ADAMS,
Senior Lead Women's Ministry Specialist, LifeWay Christian Resources

"Commencing with a babe in the bulrushes and concluding with the account of the makings of a mature marriage, the contents of *Touched by Greatness* allow you to probe the lives of women who lived in the shadow of the prince of Egypt. Dorothy Patterson exquisitely crafts literary vignettes of Jochebed, Puah and Shiphrah, Miriam, the daughter of Pharaoh, and the Egyptian sisters, along with the women of Israel and Moses' second wife, Zipporah. The vignettes encourage, edify, challenge, and motivate women of all ages, regardless of their giftedness or social status, to offer themselves as vessels to be used to glorify their heavenly Father. 'Dorothy's Dictums' and poignant prayers compel the readers of *Touched by Greatness* to investigate, integrate, and imitate the character qualities resident in the women who impacted God's chosen servant Moses. The resources for further study, teaching outlines, and inductive questions support its carefully researched, clearly articulated contents. It is a volume you will want to read, review, and use as a reference as you minister to others."

PATRICIA A. ENNIS,
Chair, Department of Home Economics-Family & Consumer Sciences,
The Master's College, Santa Clarita, California

"In this insightful and in-depth work, Dorothy Patterson helps us understand what it looked like to be a woman touched by the visionary, creative, and courageous life of Moses. Mothers, step-mothers, single sisters, wives, and friends of influential men will all relate to the importance of leading lives of influence and legacy building. Women of all walks of life will want to add this to their list of valuable resources."

JAYE MARTIN,
Director of Women's Leadership and Instructor,
The Southern Baptist Theological Seminary, Louisville, Kentucky

"Dr. Dorothy Patterson is a gifted writer who has the ability to speak to the very heart of women. In this insightful book that looks at the women who surrounded Moses, perhaps you will find a kindred spirit. Dr. Patterson paints a beautiful picture through words of women who lived in a different time period, but who faced many of today's issues."

DEBBIE BRUNSON,
Pastor's wife, First Baptist Church of Jacksonville, Florida

"Dorothy Patterson has done it again! In *Touched by Greatness*, she challenges us to look beyond the hero Moses, and imagine the lives of women who lived with a very difficult man, yet one who knew the God of the universe personally. Who were the women who nurtured, protected, admonished, and even hated this great man of God? In this rich collection of personal vignettes, insightful exegetical notes, comprehensive teaching outlines and opportunities for further study and prayer, this prolific author and woman of God has crafted an excellent resource for Bible study and personal enrichment. Dorothy Patterson has brilliantly put together the single most valuable book on the women in the life of Moses that I have read. I recommend it highly!"

ZHAVA GLASER,
Author, Adjunct Professor of Biblical Hebrew, Feinberg Center for Messianic Jewish Studies

"*Touched By Greatness* portrays the important and formative roles of women in the life of Israel's first national leader, Moses. Mrs. Patterson shares insights from several lifelong passions – in-depth Bible study, observation of the role and high value of women in society and family, and the history of God's people Israel, especially during Moses' leadership. She employs observations drawn from study and travel in Egypt and Israel to provide important details concerning daily life and customs during the historical period of the exodus. Her narrative of these historical women is made even more vivid and relevant by modern-day illustrations from the author's family and relations. The thought-provoking quotations and observations shared at the end of each chapter provide avenues for future study and group discussions."

MICHAEL H. EDENS,
Professor of Theology and Islamic Studies,
Associate Director of Institute of Christian Apologetics, Associate Dean of Graduate Studies,
New Orleans Baptist Theological Seminary, New Orleans, Louisiana

"Dr. Dorothy Patterson's thought-provoking book chronicles God's carefully crafted plan to shape the life of Moses through the women who influenced his life. Women everywhere will be inspired to be women of influence as they observe the examples of Jochebed, Miriam, and even the more obscure women who played their part in God's redemption story for the nation Israel. The inclusion of historical background, exegetical notes, teaching outlines, inductive questions and much, much more creates a valuable resource that lends itself to both individual and group study. Peruse these pages. Accept the challenge. Influence your world!"

MARGE LENOW,
Director of Women's Ministry, Bellevue Baptist Church, Cordova, Tennessee

"Dr. Dorothy Patterson has captured the essence of living a life of greatness for God, not just as the main character that He has chosen for each role in life but also as supporting participants in fulfilling His plan and purpose throughout history. Extraordinary women influenced Moses' life from the womb until His death in the wilderness, facilitating him to follow God's call on his life. Though many look at Moses as a remarkable individual, God collectively used these women in a tremendous way in the life of this great leader. From the intensely important roles of his mother, wives, and sister, to the small, unnamed players in this drama, each woman's involvement in Moses' life shaped a man called by God."

RAELENE SORITAU,
Author, songwriter, International Relations Emanuel University of Oradea, Romania.

"Few women can claim to have been profoundly touched by the greatness of so many men in her family as Dorothy Patterson can. These great men have given her much and have provided a springboard for her becoming uniquely qualified to evaluate the impact of greatness in human lives. Dorothy has once again risen to the responsibility of enriching others, especially women, from the rich reservoir of God's blessings in her life through *Touched by Greatness*. This volume is an overflow from her own life being touched by the greatness of God through the Scriptures and the lives of those she loves.

"Patterson engages the reader in fascinating vignettes closely contemplating the women whose lives were impacted in some way by the great leader, Moses. She masterfully imparts historical insights, inspiration, and instruction for women desiring to grow in wisdom serving the Lord Jesus Christ while interacting with those around them, great or small. Dorothy's scholarly excellence is entwined with enthusiasm for edifying women, encouraging and motivating them, increasing their awareness that they, too, can be used mightily of God, regardless of their backgrounds, family ties, or current circumstances. Whether women's tasks at hand are simple or splendiferous, this book invigorates the reader to execute such duties with passion while entrusting our Great and Sovereign God."

LENNIE B. KNIGHT,
Homemaker, mother, grandmother and wife of Dr. Richard Knight, Campus Physician at
Southwestern Baptist Theological Seminary, Fort Worth, Texas

"While attention has naturally focused on Moses as the deliverer of Israel, the author reminds us to slow down and carefully read each page of his life to learn the stories behind that more famous story. Dorothy Patterson reveals the creativity of God in working through women in a variety of circumstances to prepare this man of God. Every woman will perceive in these examples the potential to be used by God to influence and change another life. With a foundation of careful exegesis, readers are challenged to apply these lessons of sacrifice and courage in the context of daily decisions to influence another generation."

TAMMI LEDBETTER,
News Editor, Southern Baptist TEXAN

"Families are in crisis. A secular world seems set on robbing us of what God designed for mothers. This extensive and eloquently written work tells the inspirational stories of women who overcame major challenges and setbacks, allowing God to do the work He intended through the life of Moses. Without these women who were willing to go against the norm to protect and preserve family, Moses would not have lived to accomplish what God intended. It is absolutely one of the most fascinating books written about the significance mothers and women play in family life. As a mother-baby educator for over twenty-five years, I have witnessed the decline of the roles of mothers. We need to return to our roots and be empowered by God's design for mothering."

GLENDA EITEL,
Registered Nurse, Campus Clinic,
Southwestern Baptist Theological Seminary, Fort Worth, Texas

TOUCHED BY GREATNESS

The Women in the Life of

MOSES

Dorothy Kelley Patterson

CHRISTIAN
FOCUS

Dorothy Kelley Patterson resides with her husband Paige Patterson, the President of Southwestern Baptist Theological Seminary and a former President of the Southern Baptist Convention, at Pecan Manor in Fort Worth, Texas. She describes herself as first and foremost a homemaker, and that task has always commanded her priority in time, energies, and creativity. Patterson is a widely used free-lance writer and speaker and the author of numerous books. Currently she is Professor of Theology in Woman's Studies at Southwestern Baptist Theological Seminary.

Unless otherwise indicated, all Scripture citations are taken from the *New King James Version*. Copyright © 1982 by Thomas Nelson, Inc. Used by permission. All rights reserved.

Copyright © Dorothy Kelley Patterson 2011

ISBN 978-1-84550-631-5

10 9 8 7 6 5 4 3 2 1

Published in 2011
by
Christian Focus Publications, Ltd,
Geanies House, Fearn, Ross-shire,
IV20 1TW, Great Britain.
www.christianfocus.com

Cover design by Paul Lewis
Printed and bound by
Bell and Bain, Glasgow

Mixed Sources
Product group from well-managed forests and other controlled sources
www.fsc.org Cert no. TT-COC-002769
© 1996 Forest Stewardship Council

Contents

DEDICATED

To some men whose greatness has touched me . . .

Charles Kelley, my father
T. A. Patterson, my father-in-love
Chuck Kelley, my brother
Armour Patterson, my son
Mark Howell, my son-in-love and, most of all,
Paige Patterson, my beloved husband.

These men have overshadowed me with protection,
encircled me with tender affection,
provided me with what I have needed for sustenance,
inspired me in my spiritual journey,
and challenged me to give the Lord Jesus my best.

PREFACE

The women of the Bible have always intrigued me—their ordinary lives often fall in the midst of extraordinary challenges. When my husband was asked to be a consultant for the movie *Moses, Prince of Egypt*, I was again drawn to the women who lived in the shadow of the great lawgiver, who was marked by human weakness and yet empowered by divine calling and guidance. Through these resulting historical vignettes, my prayer is that women will be encouraged and edified, as well as challenged and motivated, to offer themselves as vessels to be used by the Lord, whether for a task as lowly as watching a basket float in the river or one as lofty as leading a host of women in praise of the one true God. Woman-to-woman ministries are the passion of my heart—not as a professional pursuit but as a service to Christ in addition to my priority commitment to manage my household, help my husband, and nurture my children and grandchildren.

This project has spanned several decades since the inspiration for its writing entered my heart and mind. As I reflected on these women, personal memories flooded my soul and my pen flowed. I am especially grateful to Tamra Hernandez, a Ph.D. student at Southwestern Baptist Theological Seminary, who has helped me with research, with gathering quotations and illustrations, and with the inductive questions included in each chapter. My administrative assistant Candi Finch, also a Ph.D. student at Southwestern, has lifted from my shoulders a myriad of details to enable me to devote time to finishing this project.

The family legacy from which I come is rich indeed and my greatest earthly blessing. My long-suffering family have allowed me to use personal experiences from our family life in my applications, and they have continually encouraged me to complete the work set before me. My gratitude overflows to all who have helped me along this journey!

Dorothy Kelley Patterson

A WORD OF EXPLANATION

Throughout this book you will find references to "The Scarlet Thread of Redemption." The whole of Scripture is devoted to the redemption provided by Jesus Christ through His atoning death on the cross. His blood sacrifice was the ransom paid for our deliverance from the penalty of sin. Rahab was responsible for extending protection to those sent out by Joshua to inspect the land. The spies in turn promised life and safety to Rahab and her household if she would hang a scarlet cord from her window, which she did (Josh. 2:21; 6:25). When Jericho and its people were destroyed, Rahab and her family were spared. The scarlet cord represented her trust in the promises of Yahweh God and testified to His faithfulness. So this "Scarlet Thread of Redemption" has woven its way through the generations and remains for every woman a reminder of God's faithfulness to all who would put their trust in Him!

Moses: A Difficult Man

As a towering personality in the history of Israel, Moses was born with neither a birth announcement nor the accompaniment of supernatural phenomena. Both Samson in the Old Testament and John the Baptist in the New Testament were distinguished by these criteria—Samson's parents (Manoah and his wife) received the word of his birth from the Angel of the Lord (Judg. 13:3, 10-11, 21, 24), and John's birth was announced to his father Zacharias (Luke 1:13) and to Mary, the relative of his mother Elizabeth (Luke 1:36). Both mothers of these prominent men in biblical history were declared barren, making their respective births an amazing blessing (Judg. 1:2; Luke 1:7). However, the birth of Moses and his rise to leadership were executed in the midst of ordinary lives and in the course of daily activities. Moses remains an enigma on the pages of history.

Although the descendant of unknown desert nomads and the son of enslaved Israelites, this uncommon man Moses, through the providence of God, was reared as a prince in Egypt. Having led his people out of Egypt, on one hand, and then into the wilderness on the other, this commoner prince could be loved and hated, embraced and rejected, admired and despised almost simultaneously! It all depended on who was living and who was dying, who was winning and who was losing.

A Hebrew born in Egypt while the Hebrews were in captivity, probably at the beginning of Egypt's eighteenth dynasty (about 1525 BC), Moses was brought up in the Egyptian royal household as the adopted son of the pharaoh's daughter, possibly the famous Hatchepsut. As the daughter of Thutmose I, Hatchepsut assumed the power of the pharaoh after the death of her brother/husband Thutmose II. She acted officially as regent but functioned as the ruler during the years her stepson Thutmose III was too young to assert himself enough to outrule her.

Although some would question the possibility of anyone with Hebrew ethnicity being allowed to grow up in Pharaoh's household, Thutmose III (1457–1425 BC) definitely brought in the princes of western Asian kings who were subject to Egypt. He wanted them to be trained in Egyptian ways before they replaced national rulers, who would die and leave open thrones. The same practice could have been in place in earlier dynasties.[1]

The most natural reading of the text indicates that the name "Moses" was assigned by Pharaoh's daughter. Names were important in the ancient world. Often the name suggested a character trait the parents envisioned for their child to pursue. Our first granddaughter was named "Abigail," meaning "the joy of the Father" (see 1 Sam. 25). It is our prayer that as she is now our joy from the heavenly Father so she will be to those who cross her path for all her life!

On the other hand, some parents may assign a name meaning the exact opposite of what they want their child to be. Such must have been the case with "Nabal," meaning "fool." Unfortunately, he lived the life of a fool, which caused his own destruction (1 Sam. 25:25).

Sometimes parents used popular names expressing their faith by joining the divine name with a noun or verb, such as "Daniel," meaning "God is my Judge," or "John," meaning "Yahweh [the personal name of God in Hebrew] has been gracious." Also the name of the child's father might be attached to his name to remind the child of his godly ancestral heritage, as in "Simon bar-Jonah," meaning "Simon, son of Jonah," or to distinguish among children with the same

---

[1] James K. Hoffmeier, *Israel In Egypt: The Evidence for the Authenticity of the Exodus Tradition* (New York: Oxford University Press, 1996), 142.

names, such as "James and John [very common names even in the time of the first century], sons of Zebedee."

Often circumstances surrounding the child's birth or some other event in his life influenced the choice of a name. Hannah named her son "Samuel" (literally "heard by God") because she asked the Lord for a son. Perhaps the name of Moses fits this category?

Although the name is associated with a Semitic root, meaning "bring" or "take out" or "remove," many scholars consider the name to be Egyptian in origin. In that case, Egyptologists define its meaning as merely "boy" or "son." The root is common in Egyptian names, such as Ahmose, Amasis, Thutmose, etc. Some suggest that the daughter of Pharaoh, who rescued the Hebrew infant from the Nile, chose the name for its Hebrew meaning; but presumably, given her own heritage, she was working from Egyptian meanings, even though she could have had some familiarity with the Hebrew language. In any case, the Bible states that she named the child Moses because she "drew him out of the water" (Exod. 2:10). This latter phrase of explanation could have merely been the inspired words passing through the author to the biblical text.

In the spiritual realm, although Moses came from the womb of a woman with faith in the God of Israel, he spent the years of his childhood among people who believed in a multitude of deities. The Egyptians worshiped gods of all shapes and forms, including the person of the pharaoh, who considered himself divine. Yet from the context of Egyptian polytheism, Moses emerged with allegiance to Hebrew monotheism, and he proclaimed his own faith commitment to the God of Israel alone. He was born into the home of a Hebrew slave; he spent his childhood and young adult years in the royal palace of Egypt; then he reclaimed his humble beginnings to identify himself with his enslaved people; finally he went down in history as the formidable leader of one of the greatest nations of antiquity—a nation that remains a power even until this modern era.

Moses began his work as a proactive seeker of justice at an early age. When he left the sheltered environment of the palace to explore the land of Egypt, he not only learned that the Israelites had been subjected to slavery in order to build garrison cities and monuments for Pharaoh, but he also observed that they had been mistreated and oppressed. This oppression probably began with the Hyksos, Egyptian pharaohs who, because of their Semitic origin, may have considered the Israelites to be their bitter enemies.

As the Hebrews rapidly increased in number, their work load was also expanded to increase their oppression and to discourage any rebellion. Moses' exile was forced because he, with righteous indignation, interfered in a labor dispute, killing an Egyptian guard who was abusing a Hebrew worker. There is no indication that Moses intended to kill the man; rather, that seems to be the tragic outcome of the confrontation. And thus the career of "the great liberator" began as he fled to the wilderness of Midian (about 1485 BC; see Acts 7:23).

Although Moses was not aware of any witnesses to the incident, other than the man he rescued, he knew the possibility that talk among the slaves would eventually put him at risk. He would be forever identified with the Hebrews of his ancestry rather than the Egyptians of his adoptive household. That would make his interference on behalf of a Hebrew man a revolutionary and treasonous act. Pharaoh did indeed put him under an edict of death. This edict of the current ruler was just as deadly as the first one issued by the pharaoh who was on the throne during Moses' infancy. He fled for his life.

Moses appeared to be a reluctant leader. He expressed humble inadequacy for the task; when approaching his people, he claimed ignorance of what to say about God; he questioned his own credibility; he maintained his lack of eloquence to speak or any charisma to move people; he confessed his own lack of self-confidence. Yet Moses showed himself from the beginning to be a man of courage and resourcefulness. He had no tinge of cowardice. The bravado and machismo that has often characterized men had been hammered into genuine courage through the "fear of the LORD" that beat within the breast of Moses. Temporal and passing boldness had been refined into permanent and abiding faith.

In expressing his reluctance to lead the Hebrews, Moses, even though he was under sentence of death in Egypt, never used his own safety as a reason for refusing to lead the people of Israel out of the land. Moses is recognized by the Hebrew people as their greatest leader, most notable prophet, and the most powerful personality in their history until the present day. The faith of Moses became the telescope by which his people could bring Yahweh God into human focus.

When plagued by rebellion, complaints, and ridicule, Moses did on occasion lose his temper, and he did experience depression and discouragement. He may have allowed his ministry duties to shortchange his family responsibilities. The text does not allude to his investment of time or attention to his wife and children and even notes lengthy periods of separation from them. This seeming neglect must have exacted a painful cost for him and for them as well. There is no evidence of loving intimacy between Moses and his wife nor any hint of tender interaction between him as a father with his children. While one dare not make dogmatic conclusions from an argument of silence, a careful reading of what is recorded in Scripture does not give positive words about Moses as husband and father. Perhaps this could serve as a warning to modern Christian leaders to set a public example of investing in their wives and children as part of their respective ministries.

The ultimate tragedy for this man, however, is that after all he endured in the forty-year trek through the wilderness, he was denied entry to the Promised Land. Disobedience is costly, even for great men. Nevertheless, the evaluation of this man, including the strength he portrayed through the providences of God, becomes more meaningful against the backdrop of his weaknesses.

When Moses returned from his exile in the wilderness of Midian to confront Pharaoh and demand the release of his people, he used different strategies to achieve his goal. He began with talking and negotiating, while continuing to stand up for what was right, refusing to back down on the assignment God had given him. However, when the talking and standing proved inadequate, he was willing to push forward whatever the cost! God used Moses to lead the people of Israel out of Egypt to freedom (about 1445 BC; see Acts 7:30).

As with any other powerful leader, the life of Moses intersected with hundreds of other lives. As with any public figure, the lives of those he touched were not always close enough to see or touch. Nevertheless, these lives were permanently changed by his presence, regardless of how they might have felt about him personally.

Through his birth family Moses' ancestry for both father and mother came through Levi, whose lineage became the priestly line, beginning with Aaron his brother (Exod. 6:16-20). Moses became a prince of Egypt via his adoption by a member of Pharaoh's household. Yet above and beyond his heritage by birth and adoption, Moses was set apart by God as a prophet. Throughout the generations, the Hebrew people have continued to honor him as their great deliverer.

This book about the women in Moses' life is based first and foremost on the facts recorded in the biblical narrative, partly on the normal course of events that would have accompanied the career of a man like Moses, and with some of my own perceptions of the feelings of these women who shared his life. The latter study on Egyptian women is much more subjective than the former but provides an insightful way to take a more personal look at the life of a very private man. Actually very few credible historical sources offer much insight into the lives of Egyptian women. In those cases where information is available, the women chronicled are from the privileged class. These tidbits from their lives are found chiseled into monuments or embedded in myths and stories. The women are identified as daughters, wives, and mothers of kings, officials, and priests.

One of the most interesting observations for a woman who looks closely at the man Moses is the fact that many of the key players in his life are women. Humanly speaking, those women must have helped to determine the events of his life. Many of the women acted courageously and defied tyranny and oppression in so doing. They were wise and resourceful in handling tough and seemingly impossible situations. Some women, a few of whom were nameless, took remarkable personal risks in order to safeguard the life of Moses when, as a baby, he must have been a typically winsome Hebrew infant.

A mother defied the orders of Pharaoh, as did the midwives who attended her during the delivery of her son. A young but precocious sister stood by in a hostile environment and dared to speak to a member of the royal family. She was a partner in a daring conspiracy that would indeed save the condemned baby boy. The daughter of Pharaoh saved a condemned child against her father's orders, engaged a slave woman to serve as his "wet nurse," and then reared the condemned child as a prince of Egypt.

Humanly speaking, without these women, there would have been no liberator for the Jews. Yet even with all that these gifted women had to offer, Moses would not have survived to lead his people without the overarching providence of God and His intervention again and again. Moses began his life under tumultuous conditions. He was born into slavery; immediately threatened by death; irrevocably torn from his birth family when he was weaned from the breast of his mother; he was adopted into Pharaoh's household and thus reared in the stronghold of the enemy. Then he was bereft of his adoptive family through a self-imposed exile. However, in moving through these adversities, God was ever present and working. Even while alone and removed from the family ties of birth and childhood, Moses was anointed by God for his mission, and God called him to the leadership of the Israelites.

Midwives, not male family members or men in the community, are mentioned in the Bible as those who dared to protect the infant Hebrew boys and let them live rather than to obey Pharaoh's edict of death. Moses' mother Jochebed, not his father, is cited as being determined to hide him rather than passively to allow him to be murdered. She kept him hidden during the first three months of his life, and she devised and executed the plan for his rescue (Exod. 2:2-3). Again, Miriam, the sister of Moses, and not his brother Aaron (who as a toddler at the time was not really a candidate for such a clandestine operation) risked her life to watch over her baby brother. She then boldly stepped forward to offer assistance to the royal princess who found the baby (Exod. 2:4, 7-8). It was a daughter, and not a son, of Pharaoh who found the infant and had enough compassion to risk the anger of Pharaoh by rescuing him (Exod. 2:5). Even Moses' wife Zipporah intervened in a divine confrontation caused by her husband's disobedience and saved his life (Exod. 4:24-26).

These women identified with Moses, especially those who were part of his household, and must have quickly learned that they were living with a difficult man. Moses moved from his position as a prince of Egypt, living within the household of Pharaoh, to become the leader of the Hebrews; but the women associated with him, with the exception of his adoptive mother, were not royalty! Each of these women, even the daughter of Pharaoh, found herself cast in Moses' shadow at some point in history; yet none was singled out by Moses for words of praise and honor.

Moses was stubborn and bold; but the most prominent women in his life were certainly not passive. He was disobedient to higher powers (i.e., Pharaoh). The women in his life were not always submissive to the authorities in their lives. In fact, one could identify the key women in Moses' life as "wild women" in a sense, for some of them did radical things, exposing themselves to danger. Yet there were those times in his life when Moses himself was more passive than proactive. He was a visionary leader; the women around him were creative and resourceful. Ultimately, Moses, as well as the women in his life, was humbled before the Creator God.

In this volume, you will have opportunity to consider what the Bible and extra-biblical sources have to say about these women who touched the life of Moses. Obviously the chapter lengths will vary according to the nature of the role each woman played in the life of Moses and the amount of information historical sources record about the woman. However, each woman is important in her own right and has a role to play in the life of Moses and within her own era of history. Each woman in some sense provides a legacy to be passed throughout the generations. The lives of these women are being viewed and, to a certain extent, evaluated by another woman. Perhaps the reader's question is this: What goes into the making of a heroine? More important to this study is the question: What equips a woman, regardless of her giftedness or station in life, to be used mightily of God?

JOCHEBED:
THE MOTHER
WHO BORE HIM

Jochebed, whose name means "honor of God" or "God is glory," was a classic Hebrew woman of faith who believed God would prevail whatever the odds. Thus she was willing to wait for His deliverance. She had clothed her faith in courage and modeled it through her works.

> By faith Moses, when he was born, *was* hidden three months by his parents, because they saw he was a beautiful child; and they were not afraid of the king's command (Heb. 11:23).

However, Jochebed was also a model mother who was committed to her part in protecting her child in the womb and bringing him into the world even under the sentence of death. But then, she was also willing to part with him and entrust his rearing to a stranger in order to ensure the saving of his life. She had faith in God's faithfulness and believed God would save her child, but she made herself available to help!

Jochebed did not appear to be depressed or despondent about the seemingly impossible task before her. After caring for and hiding the child at home for three months, she determined to entrust the safety, and even the life, of her child to God rather than continue to depend upon her own strategies for concealing the child. She faced impossible and fateful circumstances, which appeared to bring only suffering and death, but she determined to beat them. Someone has said that "mothers begin saying good-bye to their children from the moment they are born." And that was more true of Jochebed than it is for most of us. Yet she demonstrated superbly how maternal love for a child sometimes demands letting go of the child for the good of both.

Mothers face such dilemmas even today. My darling niece Sarah was released by her young, unmarried birth mother, who realized that she was not prepared for the responsibilities of motherhood. Just as a teenaged girl walked through the painful process of releasing a child, my sister Eileen was in the throes of sorrow because of irrevocable barrenness. God brought representatives of the birth mother and the adoptive mother together so that the sorrow of the mother releasing her child was mingled with the joy of the mother who would receive and nurture that precious life. The emptiness of infertility was hallowed by the joy of sacrificial unselfishness.

Whatever the dangers, Jochebed was committed to protecting her baby for the long haul. How many women have loved their babies enough to be willing to part with the baby after birth in order to give the baby life! Jochebed was willing to do what had become the best thing to do for that time! Such a sacrifice may be more difficult for a mother than putting her own life on the line to ensure her baby's safety through pregnancy and delivery. Certainly, pregnancy and childbirth have always had dangers for women. Death during childbirth was quite common in all pre-modern societies, a fact evidenced from burial sites subsequently uncovered by archaeologists.

Nothing about Jochebed appeared until she was thrust into an untenable situation. As a young wife and mother, she gave birth to her third child. Jochebed saw her child's potential and responded by doing what was necessary to assure the child's opportunity to realize his potential. Vision is as important as the courage to take action on that vision. She described this son as "beautiful" (the same Hebrew word *tov* translated elsewhere as "good"), taken to mean that he was a fine, handsome child (Exod. 2:2). Actually this observation is a reminder of the creation account found in Genesis, in which the phrase "God saw that it was good" (Hb. *tov*) occurred repeatedly. Was this birth of Moses of cosmic significance in the shadow of the creation activity of the Creator God? The Hebrew word (*tēvah*) used to identify the basket in which the baby was placed also has an interesting parallel in the account of the patriarch Noah's deliverance from the worldwide flood. That same word is used to identify the "ark" or means of rescue for Noah and his family.

HEBREW HISTORY

The Israelites had come to Egypt as invited guests. They had been welcomed by the household of Pharaoh. The term "pharaoh" (meaning "great house") is not the specific name of an Egyptian ruler but rather a general title assigned to Egyptian kings and thus used in reference to past as well as current rulers. At the time the Hebrews entered the land of Egypt, a Hebrew man named Joseph was the trusted regent for the ruling pharaoh. He had been recognized as a "savior" for Egypt after his wise planning had helped the nation prepare for a staggering famine (Gen. 45:7, 9; 50:20).

However, by the time of Jochebed, a new king, "who did not know Joseph" had arisen in Egypt, and suddenly the Israelites were not only viewed with contempt because they were foreigners but also were seen with fear because their increasing numbers were perceived as a threat to the government (Exod. 1:8–10). Rather than honored guests and welcome immigrants, the Hebrews of Jochebed's day were hated intruders and worrisome foreigners. Yet Pharaoh felt impelled to hold on to the Israelites because their slave labor had become invaluable to the Egyptians. The Hebrews were forced to do the tasks that no Egyptian wanted to do. What country would want to give up a cheap supply of foreign labor? An enormous amount of slave labor was needed to erect the monuments and architectural wonders drafted by the Egyptian ruler.

The pharaoh had settled on the edict to kill all sons born into Hebrew families in order to alleviate the perceived military threat that might develop from potential soldiers. Daughters, on the other hand, could be assimilated into the Egyptian labor force and into household service. However, Pharaoh did not realize that he was interfering with the covenant established between the promise-keeping Yahweh God and His people Israel (Gen. 12:2-3). This covenant would preclude their being wiped from the face of the earth.

UNSUNG HEROINES

Jochebed's role in history has long been understated—not an unusual lot for mothers to draw! At first glance she appears merely to be one among many in the Hebrew genealogical tables. Some would consider it chauvinistic and demeaning to identify a woman as a "wife" or "mother." Yet from all appearances, Jochebed was not only content but also honored to be a wife and mother. The seeds of love and faith Jochebed sowed in the lives of her three children certainly brought a worthy harvest.

Many other Hebrew women have been extolled, and even Jochebed's daughter Miriam has received more fame and praise throughout the centuries. Perhaps the time has come to set the record straight as to just how important Jochebed is in the life of Moses. Her conception, pregnancy, and delivery of Moses are actually overshadowed by her intelligence and resourcefulness in formulating the plan for Moses' deliverance from the jaws of death. She was a deliverer long before her son was a deliverer. At the time, she received no noteworthy adulation for her act of deliverance, nor has history been gracious to lay accolades at her feet. It is unlikely that Jochebed lived to see her son in his leadership role. She may have died while he was in the wilderness of Midian, or she could have begun the journey out of Egypt and died en route. In any case, Moses himself recorded no praise for her; yet her deeds speak for themselves very effectively. Jochebed had committed herself to service without recognition. She willingly nurtured her son even after he had been taught to honor another woman as his mother.

DEFYING PHARAOH

Jochebed's plan may not seem strategically wise. After all, the human baby is the most helpless of all young creatures and consequently demands the most care. Jochebed was not unaware that she was taking a chance with the life of her infant son. However, she must have been cognizant that the gathering of women to wash clothes or draw water along the banks of the Nile would not be unusual. This gathering would provide a natural cover to execute her daring plan. Out of bulrushes she fashioned a cradle/basket large enough for the child to rest comfortably, and then she caulked the basket with pitch and bitumen to make it waterproof.

DID YOU KNOW?

The material used to fashion the cradle was from the papyrus plant, technically the Cyperus papyrus, *which once grew abundantly in the marshlands of the Nile Delta. The Egyptians used the plant for a variety of purposes—they used it to record letters; to make sandals, cording, and even in the construction of boats (see Isa. 18:2; Job 9:20).*

Having finished crafting the basket, Jochebed placed the precious cargo in it and set it afloat on the Nile River under the eye of her watchful daughter, leaving the preservation of her child to the providence of God. In so doing she appeared to be obeying Pharaoh's order, but actually she was defying his edict of death just as did the midwives who had delivered her son alive. Jochebed knew that the popularity of the river would be an attraction for someone to come, and divine providence could bring the person who might find and rescue the baby.

In her own strength, Jochebed could not have stepped out in faith with such confidence. For one would expect a baby floating on the river to cry. In this hostile environment, one would expect a crying baby would attract attention. Logically, an Egyptian soldier would have followed the cries and killed the baby. But, in this case, the providence of God ultimately controlled the events. The basket was sighted by a member of the royal family, and one of Pharaoh's daughters, with her curiosity aroused, sent a maiden to retrieve the basket (Exod. 2:5). Only when she opened the basket did the baby cry, awakening the maternal compassions of the princess, who instantly decided to risk the ire of her father and save the baby boy.

What a unique father/daughter duo! The father was the greatest enemy of the Hebrew people, seeking their destruction through the despicable means of infanticide. The daughter became a savior to the Hebrews, rescuing the one who was to become their deliverer! At this point one has to consider the reliability of Scripture in a different light. If the Bible is merely a myth or tradition, why would the Israelites have chosen to weave a story of their salvation as coming from their hated enemy—Egypt?

WET NURSES

Jochebed's maternal responsibility did not end when she placed her son in the basket and set it afloat on the river. In the providence of God and through the alert intervention of her daughter, Jochebed was hired by the Egyptian princess to breastfeed her own son, whom she had earlier set adrift in the Nile! Miriam wisely appeared indifferent with her proposal to find a wet nurse, and she did not identify Jochebed as the baby's mother, knowing the adoptive mother would never have agreed to such a proposal.

In addition, Jochebed must have had great self-control to appear before the princess and make a business arrangement to assume the position of "wet nurse" to this new addition to the royal court. She did not show her unique maternal bonding with this special child. Yet through these months of succoring the child at her own breast, Jochebed must have used every means to link herself to her son—her voice, her touch, perhaps even her body scent, which she could have made unique through the use of perfume or spices.

My husband and I have two darling granddaughters. I remember watching our daughter Carmen begin bonding with these precious ones even before their birth. Because her mother walked the treadmill daily until the day of delivery and because the family pet barked regularly at all activity, our older granddaughter Abigail was familiar with these routine activities and was undisturbed and even comforted when her mother would strap her tiny frame to her own body and walk the treadmill. From the first time I cradled Abigail, and later Rebekah, in my arms, I have been careful to help each of our little girls grow accustomed to my face, my voice, a song repeated again and again, a single signature fragrance. Jochebed must have used all human senses to bind herself to her son.

Women identified as "wet nurses" in the Bible were accorded great esteem. Rebekah's nurse was buried under a terebinth tree, designated as '*Allon Bakuth* (literally "Terebinth of Weeping," Gen. 35:8), and Joash's nurse hid and cared for him at risk of her own life until Joash was old enough to become king (2 Kings 11:1-3).

Although a bit unusual in the Western world in this generation, being a wet nurse is a role with which I can readily identify. When our daughter Carmen was born in the Southern Baptist Hospital in New Orleans, Louisiana, April 10, 1970, she soon developed trauma in the form of Hyaline Membrane Disease.

Although this condition is effectively treated now, at that time it was most often fatal. As our baby was clinging to life via the respirator in the hope that her lungs would be cleared of the life-threatening mucus, I had been advised that her chance of survival would be enhanced by breastfeeding.

This unique mother-to-baby nurture had been in my plans all along, not only because of my own medical history of allergies and asthma but also because of the satisfying experience I had enjoyed with my firstborn child. The physical closeness and spiritual bonding that began with the duty of breastfeeding had been implanted in my heart and soul as a mother's privilege I did not want to miss!

Breast pumps were available but very painful and not too effective. No man–made machine does the job like the manufacturer's time-proven method of another living creation who clears all the milk ducts simultaneously with his effective sucking action!

In the ancient world, the vast majority of women breastfed their own babies. Mother's milk was regarded as essential to sustaining the life of a newborn baby and was also used as an important ingredient in some prescriptions. In the event a mother could not or would not nurture her child, a "wet nurse" was employed. When a mother's own milk failed, when the mother died, if a mother wanted to conceive again quickly and felt breastfeeding might delay that conception, or when a mother simply chose not to do so, another plan had to be implemented. A wet nurse was a woman who had given birth to her own child, who might have died, or perhaps she chose to feed two children at once.

As the life of my own baby girl hung in the balance, my gynecologist came to me with an unusual proposal: Would you consider being a "wet nurse" for another baby until your daughter can be removed from the respirator? Sometimes a mother is not physically able to nurse her own child. In some parts of the world even today, this crisis means that a wet nurse, usually another nursing mother, must be secured to feed the baby her own breast milk. My physician told me later that he never expected me to breastfeed my own baby, since there was little chance of her survival; but he thought my preoccupation with another baby would give my body a chance for healing from the surgical procedure through which I had gone to deliver my daughter. Another of his patients was the wife of a seminary student who had been our classmate. When the family found out about our sorrow and expressed a desire to help and when that mother experienced a spinal headache and could not thus receive her baby immediately, the doctor, unmarried and never having had children of his own, made his unusual and unorthodox proposal. We accepted, and I put this tiny boy to my breast to provide his nourishment for the first few days of his life and to protect a supply of that unique nourishment for our precious daughter—should she survive.

The doctor was right! Instead of dwelling on my own sorrows and suffering as well as physical discomfort from using the breast pump, my attention was somewhat diverted as I concentrated on proper rest and nourishment for myself in order to be a conduit of sustenance for the baby (nature's natural and most effective breast pump!) briefly entrusted to my care. In the wake of the prayers of God's people and His merciful providence, my baby girl, too, experienced deliverance from what seemed certain death! Within three days, Carmen was suckling my breast and gradually gaining her strength and health.[1]

"Wet nurses" were widely accepted within royal households. Most royals considered the responsibility of nursing a child an inconvenience or annoyance. Some may have considered it more prestigious to use a wet nurse than to feed their babies themselves.

The princess must have had the baby's nourishment quickly brought to her mind by the crying. She then moved to meet the need of the child, providentially reinforced by Miriam's suggestion. God's providence did not stop with Miriam's interjection and the response from the princess, for much more was involved in being a wet nurse than putting the child to the breast. Not only did the breast provide milk as

---

[1] As a postscript to this personal vignette, I remember a subsequent encounter and follow-up to this memorable experience in my life. A young adult man with a winsome smile approached me and asked, "Do you know who I am?" When he gave me his name, indeed I did know who he was. How delighted I was to be able to express my personal gratitude to one who served as an encouragement to me in a dark hour and one who helped me prepare in the most natural way for sustaining the life of my daughter.

nourishment for the newborn baby, but it also was designed to be a source for bonding between mother and baby. The prophet described this bonding as "the consolation of her bosom" (see Isa. 66:11).

Jochebed's love had no strings attached. She had to bid farewell to her son much sooner than is expected for a mother. When other mothers were cradling their children who had not been condemned to death, Jochebed was making provisions to release her son. In giving up her son, Jochebed offered Moses to the Lord and, in a sense, to the world. If she had tried to hold back her son in his infancy, she would likely have lost him to premature death, and the Hebrews would not have had his leadership.

Breastfeeding in ancient times, usually continued until approximately age three. It was a time of special commitment on the part of the mother or "wet nurse" because she was tied to her baby in a unique way. In the case of Jochebed, she did not have to come to the palace to nurse the baby; rather, the princess directed her to take the child away. Again, by the providences of God, Moses spent these earliest and very formative years in the home of his parents, suckled and nurtured by his own wise and resourceful mother.

Perhaps Jochebed told Moses the story of Joseph. Is it coincidence that twenty-five percent of the book of Genesis is about Joseph, or is that the result of Moses' time at his mother's knee? Only after his weaning was Moses returned to the palace to be reared by his adoptive mother in the household of Pharaoh (Exod. 2:8-10). The child's time as a "suckling" (the term used to designate a nursing infant) was brief, even if the nursing continued, as often was the case, until the child was two or three years old.

The weaning was a milestone in the child's life, a sign of crossing the line from infancy to childhood. However, even after the return of Moses at such a young and vulnerable age to the Egyptian royal household, all the learning of the Egyptians could not blot out what his mother Jochebed had taught him during the months he spent in her care.

JOCHEBED'S RISK

Many would question Jochebed's putting her infant son at risk in the waters of the Nile with its predators within and the uncertainties lurking upon its shores. Knowing the cruel decree that sealed the child's doom, why not accept the inevitable and end the child's life in a humane fashion. Wasn't she practicing infanticide at its worse by putting her helpless child in the hands of the elements of nature? Would it have been more noble to keep the child at home until discovered by the authorities and then clutch the child to her breast and die with the child? Would it have been wiser to distance herself from the newborn son in order to preserve her own life and rear her two older children? After all, she did have a daughter and another son who were dependent upon her for protection and care in the cruel and perilous environment in which they lived.

You can easily second-guess this independent and bold woman. You can judge her motives and question her judgment. However, I find myself intrigued by her creative strategy and unshakable faith in the God of Israel. What she ultimately did was to entrust her helpless son to the domain that was uniquely God's. The river—its currents and course; the weather—its temperature, moisture; the creatures that might inhabit its waters or banks—all these factors must have been considered by this resourceful mother.

Jochebed was a woman with a daring plan. The basket in which she placed the child was tightly woven and carefully caulked so as to make it waterproof and then fitted with a covering to disguise its contents. She must have planned the timing of the basket's release just as carefully. Had she observed a regular pattern among the women in the royal household when approaching the water for their bathing rituals? Had she even noted a particular daughter of Pharaoh who seemed more compassionate than the other women of the royal entourage? These questions to contemplate yield no methodical answers. Jochebed could have simply moved through her plan with an unseen Mover prodding her along.

She may have not known from one moment to the next what she would do, but rather she may have submitted herself to be a servant in the hands of the Almighty, directed step by step to accomplish His purposes.

Having studied the recorded events and observations, I have envisioned Jochebed as somewhere between mechanical movement and spontaneous spurts of action. I believe that Jochebed was moved by a Supreme Power, the one called Yahweh by the Hebrews, the God of the universe. Even if a mere mortal—man or woman—could have come up with a plan like she envisioned, it would have been superfluous without God's providential intervention along the way. Nevertheless, God's appointment of Jochebed to be the mother of Israel's deliverer was no mere coincidence. She was divinely anointed for her assignment just as surely as Moses was for his. The maternal mantle on the capable shoulders of Jochebed inspired her to apply her full energies to the task of motherhood. She also used her keen intellect, wise intuitions, and unusual creativity. She was bound by an unflinching commitment to the task of preserving the life of her son. This woman not only had to come up with a plan, but she also had to be daring enough to execute that plan.

For every mother, Jochebed gives a picture of strength and courage to continue in the daily tasks of motherhood despite whatever may attempt to distract her. Mothers find themselves ready to catch the tears of sorrow as well as the moments of joy in this awesome task.

A MOTHER'S INFLUENCE

How can a mother influence her children? After all, someone has echoed the prophet Ezekiel ("Like mother, like daughter!" Ezek. 16:44) with the words, "Children are the reflection of their mother." How can a mother teach her child anything she herself is not, and how can her children become anything other than what she has lived before them? The best teachers always live what they teach since the influence of an exemplary life carries far more weight than mere words.

When a mother breaks a promise to her child, the child is not inspired to truthfulness. When a mother brags about short-changing the grocer, she is not making integrity a part of her child's character. When a mother publicly belittles and berates her child, she is not teaching her child gentleness. When a mother easily loses her temper, she should not expect a child marked by self-control.

In a volume entitled *The Birds' Christmas Carol*, an un-educated mother is trying to teach her children proper social behavior for a party to which they had been invited. Despite her drills in polite phrases and proper table etiquette, the mother is greatly discouraged at how little they have retained. She finally blurts out in despair, "… if folks would only say, 'Oh, childern [*sic*] will be childern!' But they won't. They'll say, … 'who fetched them childern up?'"[1]

How emblazoned on the heart of every mother is this simple insight! Often your children say more about you in the living of their lives than you want to hear. Being a mother is an honor, but even more than that—it is an awe-some responsibility!

What made Jochebed a great mother? First, she was a woman of vision; she saw possibilities for her child. She taught him values before he was taken from her. Second, she was a woman of creativity. When all the odds were against her, she refused to give up! She knew that the light that would shine furthest must shine brightest at home. Third, she was a woman of courage who was willing to make personal sacrifices because she was a woman of faith. Her resourcefulness enabled her to nourish her baby.

God filled her quiver with "arrows," and Jochebed refused to consider any of those arrows to be errors (Ps. 127)! Despite the personal risk or even inconvenience of having children in her circumstances, Jochebed was determined to protect the lives God entrusted to her. She introduced her son to the faith of Yahweh God with dedication and urgency from the

---

[1] Kate Douglas Wiggin, *The Bird's Christmas Carol* (Boston & New York: Houghton Mifflin, 1912), 66-67.

earliest days of his life. The faith of Jochebed lived in the life of her son Moses, and surely her steadfast faith has inspired countless mothers throughout the generations!

PRAYER

Heavenly Father, please look into my mother's heart. Give me sacrificial love for children. Awaken my creativity and generate my energies to enable me to nurture, encourage, and edify these young ones whom I love so much. Fill me with your wisdom and discernment so that I can effectively influence each of them, turning their hearts to God and building their characters within.

FURTHER STUDY

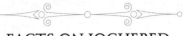

FACTS ON JOCHEBED

- *Name:* Jochebed – a Hebrew name that is pronounced *Yokheved*
- *Scripture References:* Exodus 2:1-10; 6:20; Numbers 26:59; Hebrews 11:23-29
- *Family:* Descendant of Levi; Wife of Amram; Mother of Miriam, Aaron, and Moses
- *Occupation:* Homemaker
- *Spiritual Gifts:* mercy, wisdom, knowledge, faith, discernment
- *Characteristics:* intelligence, creativity, determination, selflessness, courage, boldness
- *Dates:* Exodus – 1445 BC. This date is commonly accepted by evangelical theologians and historians.

    Birth: *c.* 1555

    Marriage: *c.* 1537

    Birth of Children: Miriam *c.* 1535 BC; Aaron *c.* 1528 BC; Moses *c.* 1525 BC.

EXEGETICAL NOTES

Exodus 2:1 "the family of Levi"

The marriage of Jochebed and Amram may have been arranged, but they accepted one another with a strong commitment. This served as the foundation for a family who would serve the LORD despite overwhelming opposition.

Exodus 2:2 "she saw that he was beautiful"

"Beautiful" (Hb. *tov*, "good") is the same word used in the creation account to express satisfaction with the divine handiwork (Gen. 1:4, 10, 18, 25, 31). The expression was a natural one for a mother to use in describing her child.

Exodus 2:6 "felt sorry for him"

This natural expression of a woman's nurturing, maternal spirit (Hb. *chamal*, "have compassion on, be mild and gentle, treat with tenderness") comes to her as the DNA of creation and will sometimes manifest itself in unexpected ways.

Exodus 2:9 "took the boy and nursed him"

Breastfeeding is the natural means planned by the Creator to forge an irrevocable bond between a mother and her child. This providential intervention gave the opportunity for physical and emotional bonding between Moses and his godly mother, giving to him immersion in her faith and values in his earliest, formative years.

Exodus 2:10 "he became her son"

There is no explanation in the text as to how the daughter of Pharaoh secured her father's permission to bring a condemned Hebrew baby boy into the royal court and rear him as a prince of Egypt. However, she was faithful to her commitment to adopt the baby and make him her own, which she first affirmed publicly by naming him. "She named him Moses," saying, "Because I drew him out of the water."

The name itself may be a means of emphasizing the bicultural heritage of Moses since both the Hebrew and Egyptian languages have possible etymological roots associated with it. Whether Pharaoh's daughter chose the name because of the wordplay involving both languages or because she was reliving the child's rescue from death in the river is a question to ponder but does not affect the meaning of the text.

PARALLEL REFERENCES

Exodus 6:20

Now Amram took for himself Jochebed, his father's sister, as wife; and she bore him Aaron and Moses. And the years of the life of Amram were one hundred and thirty-seven.

Numbers 26:59

The name of Amram's wife was Jochebed, the daughter of Levi, who was born to Levi in Egypt: and to Amram she bore Aaron and Moses and their sister Miriam.

Hebrews 11:23-29

By faith Moses, when he was born, was hidden three months by his parents, because they saw he was a beautiful child; and they were not afraid of the king's command. By faith Moses, when he became of age, refused to be called the son of Pharaoh's daughter, choosing rather to suffer affliction with the people of God than to enjoy the passing pleasures of sin, esteeming the reproach of Christ greater riches than the treasures in Egypt; for he looked to the reward. By faith he forsook Egypt, not fearing the wrath of the king; for he endured as seeing Him who is invisible. By faith he kept the Passover and the sprinkling of blood, lest he who destroyed the firstborn should touch them. By faith they passed through the Red Sea as by dry land, whereas the Egyptians, attempting to do so, were drowned.

TEACHING OUTLINE

INTRODUCTION

Jochebed is described as "a daughter of Levi" (Exod. 2:1) to indicate her family connections to the priestly line. The tribe of Levi was charged with handing down the traditions of Abraham among the Israelites. Jochebed's husband Amram had the same family heritage.

Jochebed will be remembered as a courageous and determined woman of faith because of her selfless act of heroism in circumventing the edict of death Pharaoh placed on her son. She did indeed put him in the Nile as the tyrant had demanded (Exod. 1:22), but she chose to place her baby in a carefully fashioned ark of safety and cunningly to coincide his release to the river with the visit of the royal women. All was to be stealthily monitored by her watchful daughter.

This resourceful mother left no stone unturned in her efforts to assure the safety of her baby son. She is remembered even today through the lives of her children. Moses delivered the Israelites and continues to be recognized as Israel's foremost leader in the annals of history. Aaron was a co-laborer with Moses in securing the Israelites' deliverance from Egypt and became the nation's first High Priest, charged with representing the people before God. Miriam—prophetess, musician, and poet—is noted as the leader of the Hebrew women in her lifetime. Perhaps the foremost common ingredient in their lives is the godly heritage of their mother.

I.   The Faith of a Mother (Exod. 2:1-10)
    A. The Gift of Life (vv. 1-2)
    B. The Responsibility of Nurture (vv. 3-9)
    C. The Reward of Sacrifice (v. 10)

II. The Faith of the Son (Heb. 11:23-29)
    A. Modeled by Parents (v. 23)
    B. Attacked by Forces of Evil (vv. 24-26)
    C. Lived Out in Personal Commitment (vv. 27-29)

CONCLUSION

Jochebed risked her life to secure the physical safety of her children, and she nurtured them in the Lord, building character within to equip them for the spiritual tasks they would pursue in adulthood. Nurturing children in the love and service of God can influence a whole nation for good.

QUOTATIONS

"For the hand that rocks the cradle / Is the hand that rules the world." William Ross Wallace

"As a mother, you should consider your child your greatest disciple." Dorothy Patterson

"Courage is resistance to fear, mastery of fear—not absence of fear." Mark Twain, *Pudd'nhead Wilson*, chapter 12.

"When one does not love too much one does not love enough." Blaise Pascal

"There is always one moment in childhood when the door opens and lets the future in." Graham Greene, *The Power and the Glory* (New York: Penguin, 1940), 12.

"The mother's heart is the child's school-room." Nineteenth-century preacher Henry Ward Beecher

ILLUSTRATIONS

MONICA, THE MOTHER OF AUGUSTINE

"Monica, the devout mother of Saint Augustine, prayed fervently for her son's salvation. But Augustine's non-Christian father was as zealous to lead Augustine into sin as Monica was to introduce him to Christ—and Augustine showed little spiritual interest . . . After he became a Christian, Augustine wrote in prayer of his indebtedness to his mother's intercession: 'And now didst thou "stretch forth thy hand from above" and didst draw up my soul out of that profound darkness because my mother, thy faithful one, wept to thee on my behalf more than mothers are accustomed to weep for the bodily deaths of their children.' [from *Augustine's Confessions* 3.11.19, trans. Albert C. Outler]." Jean Fleming, *A Mother's Heart: A Look at the Values, Vision, and Character for the Christian Mother*, rev. ed. (Colorado Springs: NavPress, 1996), 104–5.

"She served her husband as her master, and did all she could to win him for You, speaking to him of You by her conduct, by which You made her beautiful . . . Finally, when her husband was at the end of his earthly span, she gained him for You."

"I was a believer like all my household, except father: but he could not cancel in me the rights of my mother's piety . . . . For she tried earnestly, my God, that You should be my father, not him." Augustine, *Confessions* 9.9.19-22.

THE MOTHER OF HUDSON TAYLOR

"...on a Saturday afternoon in 1849, another mother prayed for the salvation of her only son, Hudson Taylor: 'Leaving her friends she went alone to plead with God for his salvation. Hour after hour passed while that mother was still upon her knees, until her heart flooded with a joyful assurance that her prayers were heard and answered.'

"When Mrs. Taylor returned home, her son told her of his conversion. Hudson Taylor later founded the China Inland Mission. He ministered to countless Chinese, and his example has inspired thousands of missionaries. His life still speaks today to those who have been deeply challenged by his devotion to Christ." Jean Fleming, *A Mother's Heart: A Look at the Values, Vision, and Character for the Christian Mother*, rev. ed. (Colorado Springs: NavPress, 1996), 105; quote from Dr. and Mrs. Howard Taylor, *Hudson Taylor's Spiritual Secret* (Chicago: Moody Press, China Inland Mission edition, 1958), 13.

SUSANNA WESLEY, MOTHER OF JOHN WESLEY

"Mrs. Wesley was a quietly practical woman, who, having much to do, found time to do everything, by dint of unflagging energy and industry and a methodical habit of mind." As soon as her oldest son "began to talk she began to instruct him."

When her daughter Hetty was five years old, "Mrs. Wesley began to keep regular school with her family for six hours a day, and kept it up, for twenty years, with only the few unavoidable interruptions caused by successive confinements, and a fire at the Rectory.

"How patiently she taught was shown when, one day, her husband had the curiosity to sit by and count while she repeated the same thing to one child more than twenty times. 'I wonder at your patience,' said he; 'you have told that child twenty times that same thing.' 'If I had satisfied myself by mentioning it only nineteen times,' she answered, 'I should have lost all my labour. It was the twentieth time that crowned it.'"Eliza Clarke, *Susanna Wesley* (London: W. H. Allen & Co., 1886), 25, 27-28.

DOROTHY'S DICTUM FOR MOTHERS

I. Vision—see your child's possibilities

II. Creativity—never give up

III. Courage—be willing to make personal sacrifices

INDUCTIVE QUESTIONS

1. What can a contemporary mother learn from Jochebed? Discuss character qualities/lifestyle to emulate.

2. Describe different ways in which a mother can be selfish.

3. Draw a word picture of Jochebed's motherhood that can be emulated by modern mothers.

4. Can you think of other noteworthy biblical mothers? Compose a list of their characteristics for your contemplation.

5. Write a personal letter to some mother you appreciate to encourage and affirm her sacrificial ministries.

6. Prepare a genealogical chart as a guide for studying your own heritage.

7. Make your own list of the most important lessons you would teach your child.

THE SCARLET THREAD OF REDEMPTION

Jochebed embraced the faith of Yahweh, the one true living God, for herself. She sought and accepted the providences of a faith journey, believing God could provide deliverance from death and sustain life. She faithfully nurtured her children spiritually as well as physically, passing on to the next generation not only how to be rightly related to God but also how to live by His principles even in the midst of overwhelming adversities.

PUAH AND SHIPHRAH: THEIR RESPECT FOR LIFE SPARED HIM

Puah, whose name means "girl," and Shiphrah, whose name means "beautiful one," were either Hebrew midwives or foreigners who were midwives to the Hebrews. These two women may have been supervising a team of midwives, or they may have been two women who distinguished themselves before the LORD for their protection of life. Their ethnic origin has been the source of debate among Jewish scholars for many centuries. Although their names are common northwest Semitic names, Josephus, the Jewish historian (AD 37–100), argues effectively that they were not Hebrews and that Shiphrah and Puah were Egyptian women hired by Pharaoh to carry out his decree to kill all male Hebrew babies. Others argue that they must have been Hebrews since they defied Pharaoh himself. However, that argument is discarded since the daughter of Pharaoh obviously disobeyed him.

Some rabbis have even suggested that the midwives were actually Jochebed and Miriam (the mother and sister of Moses). The latter is hardly tenable. There would be no reason for the Bible to assign pseudonyms to conceal the identity of these two heroines who were so worthy of praise.

Since it would be highly unlikely for an Egyptian ruler to depend on mothers of Israel to kill children of other mothers of Israel, I tend to believe that these were Semitic women, probably members of another non-Hebrew, lower-class group who were residing in

Egypt. These women were likely to have served the Hebrew community professionally as midwives—whether on request of the Hebrew women or at the insistence of the pharaoh, who wanted to use these women as angels of death.

On the other hand, with the number of children being born, the Hebrew women may have needed assistance from the large number of Egyptian midwives, who may also have had better access to supplies needed to ensure a safe birth. Since the Bible mentions that the midwives contrasted the Hebrew women with the Egyptian women in childbirth, they must have also served women who were not Hebrews, further proof that they were not Israelites but Egyptians or from some other Mesopotamian group residing in Egypt.

The edict of Pharaoh did not affect female babies since they would be considered helpless against Egypt. They also would provide useful field and household service and could even be assimilated into the Egyptian culture through marriage.

In a culture that prepared so diligently for the afterlife and that gave such importance to names, interestingly the name of the ruling pharaoh is not recorded in the biblical account.

DID YOU KNOW?

A prominent part of the ancient Egyptian monuments is the cartouche bearing the name of the ruling pharaoh. A cartouche is like a nameplate, enclosing in an oval the hieroglyphs denoting the royal person's name. When they were in Egypt, Napoleon's soldiers used this French word for the shapes, which reminded them of "gun cartridges" or bullets. The nickname eventually became the standard term. In fact, often a new ruler would set out to deface the cartouche of his predecessors on monuments. He would then put his own cartouche or name on the monuments throughout the land.

However, despite the omission of the pharaoh's name, the names of the midwives are recorded in Scripture as a reminder, even until now, that they were faithful to do their part in God's plan for delivering and preserving His people.

This commitment is particularly significant if the women were not Hebrews and did not have a national commitment to add to their spiritual sensitivities for honoring the sanctity of life. After all, one did not, then or now, have to be a Hebrew to fear God and act morally.

These midwives did indeed fear Yahweh God of Israel. They evidently had already been exposed to the superiority of the God worshiped by the monotheistic Hebrews. Perhaps they intuitively knew that the God of Israel must be more powerful than the king, who declared himself to be divine and part of the pantheon of Egyptian gods. For whatever reasons, these midwives risked their lives by refusing to comply with Pharaoh's demand to murder the infant Hebrew sons.

MIDWIFERY IN ANCIENT TIMES

Midwifery was one of the few professions open to women in Egypt, and those who identified themselves with this profession seem to have been well respected. Often a friend or neighbor of the family served as the midwife. Generally the midwife was a mother herself. She had learned by personal experience what kind of help was needed in the delivery.

The "neighbor women" who attended Ruth during the birth of her son even named Ruth's son Obed (Ruth 4:17). Other midwives are mentioned in the Bible. For example, Rachel had a midwife at the birth of Benjamin (Gen. 35:17), as did Tamar at the birth of her twins (Gen. 38:28). Apparently, in addition to attending the mother during her travail at birth, the midwife also cut the umbilical cord, washed the baby, rubbed its skin with salt, and then swaddled it (Ezek. 16:4). She completed her responsibilities by placing the baby at the mother's breast and announcing his safe arrival to the father. In addition to these tasks, the midwife often encouraged and coached the mother during the delivery.

A mother delivered her child without the benefit of pain-killers or sophisticated medical assistance. The delivery was often painful and difficult and, in some cases, life-threatening. The baby, too, came into the world in a less than ideal setting. Home birth often occurred in the midst of unsanitary conditions—dirt floors, polluted water, contaminated swaddling clothes, and disease-ridden animals as well as flies inhabiting the same quarters. Studies have indicated an unusually high infant mortality rate.

DID YOU KNOW?

In ancient societies, the mother would lie down to deliver a child or squat in a crouching position. The "birthstool," literally translated from the Hebrew word as "the two stones," was another interesting part of the birth process. The woman would assume a crouching or sitting position on this stool when the labor pains became more intense and time had come for the baby's birth (see 1 Sam. 4:19).

THE MIDWIVES' RISK

The midwives attending Jochebed must have been wise women with a large measure of creativity in their arsenals. Their consciences would not allow them to move from being forerunners of life to pallbearers of death. Perhaps their refusal to murder the Hebrew male children was the first recorded act of civil disobedience in protest for a moral cause. In any case, it was rare. Most who live under tyrannical dictatorships decide to "go along to get along." They are willing to obey even immoral laws in order to protect or to advance themselves in the ruling hierarchy. Certainly there are still open wounds from such compliance with the immoral genocide of the Jews, as well as many other human beings believed to be "expendable," in Germany during World II, not to mention the open slaughter of particular people groups in the Soviet Union, Bosnia, and not a few African nations.

Puah and Shiphrah were not looking for martyrdom; they did not defy Pharaoh in a prideful way. Rather, they were ready with what may be described as a humble explanation or witty response when Pharaoh demanded reasons for their lack of compliance to his edict to murder the male babies as they came from the womb. In that explanation they were careful not to blame the Hebrew women, which would have placed the Hebrews in an even more serious situation. Their explanation that the Hebrew women delivered their babies too quickly was believable enough to provide a reasonable explanation (Exod. 1:19).

First and foremost, these women must have held a high view of life, a respect for the Creator, and a determination to link hands with God in extending the generations. Sometimes contemporary health professionals are willing to give up too quickly. I remember receiving a call from one of the young men who had served as a pastoral student intern for my husband. He was then pastor of his own congregation in southeast Texas. His wife had given birth to a fine son. The physician attending her had unwisely encouraged her not to continue breastfeeding her newborn son. Unfortunately, her infant son was allergic to and thus rejected every artificial formula combination they could concoct.

When I received the call of distress in Dallas, there seemed no hope that the baby would survive. I hurriedly gathered up my own two young children, loaded the car, including books from my library on breastfeeding, and headed for Dallas. Immediately I contacted the national offices for the La Leche League, and their staff went into action. Within hours, we located nursing mothers who agreed to express extra milk from their own breasts to send to the dying infant. We used that milk to keep the baby alive. Meantime we began the painstaking process of relactating the mother. Within days, the mother's milk supply returned, and the baby regained strength. The baby is now a godly businessman—married and rearing his own children.

Women have unique intuitions and extraordinary creativity to enable them to fight for life in a committed way. Puah and Shiphrah are worthy examples of women who coupled their training and creativity with their determination in order to accomplish what seemed to be impossible!

The question arises: Where did these lowly women get the courage to disobey Pharaoh's orders, knowing that in so doing their lives would be in danger? The Bible records that they "feared God." Certainly one would hope that consciousness of the existence of a Higher Power who makes moral demands on human beings would constitute the ultimate restraint on evil as well as provide the supreme incentive for good.

The real motivation of the midwives for protecting the babies from the decree of death came because they feared God more than Pharaoh (Exod. 1:17), and their fear of God seemed to liberate them from what surely would have been understood as a natural fear of the oppressive Pharaoh. Their noncompliance with Pharaoh's law came because of the irreconcilable conflict in their own hearts between obedience to a depraved law and their own God-fearing allegiance to the higher moral law of God.

As a result of their personal courage and commitment to God's law, these women were rewarded with "households" from God (Exod. 1:21). They had a part in preserving the ancestry of the priests, kings, and princes of Israel.

PRAYER

Heavenly Father, instill within me the courage to do right whatever the cost. Don't let me be content to hover over my own household with no regard for community and nation. Keep within me a respect for life. You are the Creator of all; you control life and death. Raise up women like Puah and Shiphrah who will use every means at their disposal to protect innocent life.

FURTHER STUDY

FACTS ON PUAH AND SHIPHRAH

- *Names:* Puah and Shiphrah
- *Scripture References:* Exodus 1:15–22
- *Occupation:* Health professionals, namely, midwives
- *Spiritual Gifts:* Mercy, discernment, wisdom, knowledge
- *Dominant Characteristics:* Courage, intelligence, resourcefulness, integrity
- *Timeline:* The lives of the midwives were probably parallel to Jochebed's since they overlapped at the birth of Jochebed's son

EXEGETICAL NOTES

Exodus 1:17, 21 "the midwives feared God"

"Midwives" (Hb. *yalad*, "bearing young, bringing forth life or doing work of a midwife," i.e., assisting in ushering in new life) are referenced seven times in this passage and two other times in the Old Testament (Gen. 35:17; 38:28).

"Feared" (Hb. *yarē'*, "apprehending danger; feeling your own weakness; venerating as with spiritual reverence, motivating worship and honor") appears twice in this passage (Exod. 1:17, 21). Thus, their "fear" of God (v. 17) became the reason for their reward (v. 21). Certainly elsewhere in the Old Testament "the fear of the LORD" is credited as the starting point for attaining wisdom (Prov. 1:7). In any case, this "fear" took the focus of these midwives away from their personal goals and placed their attention on God.

Exodus 1:19 "the Hebrew women . . . are lively"

"Lively" (Hb. *chayeh*, "vigorous or robust") is a *hapax legomenon*, i.e., a word that appears only once in Scripture. The word may simply refer to the fact that the Hebrew women were more active than the Egyptian women during childbirth. The greater "liveliness" of the Hebrew women may have been a cultural/ethnic difference or the result of the difficult circumstances of their lives as a minority race and enslaved people in Egypt.

Exodus 1:21 "He provided households for them" "Households" (Hb. *bayith*, "house or palace") here is a reference to families. They would conceive their own children and build a familial legacy. This blessing was not the result of their ingenuity or even the reward of saving babies per se. Rather their reward came as a direct fruit of the their obedience, even when their own lives were at risk. They "feared God"!

PARALLEL REFERENCES
Genesis 35:17
Now it came to pass, when she was in hard labor, that the midwife said to her, "Do not fear; you will have this son also."

Genesis 38:28
And so it was, when she was giving birth, that the one put out his hand; and the midwife took a scarlet thread and bound it on his hand, saying, "This one came out first."

TEACHING OUTLINE
INTRODUCTION
Puah and Shiphrah were heroines and women to whom one can look for guidance in determining differences between right and wrong. They have distinguishing character qualities that women today should emulate. Whether they were indeed leaders of a large group of midwives or merely employed as midwives, they illustrate qualities of leadership. Not only were their names recorded in Holy Scripture but an account of their confrontation with Pharaoh must have been widely circulated

and talked about in households throughout Egypt. Don't you think that every woman who has given birth would have loved to have one of these women to attend her?

I. In Their Hands, the Midwives Held the Power of Life and Death (Exod. 1:16).

II. In Their Hearts, the Midwives Feared God (v. 17).

III. With their Actions, the Midwives Pursued Creativity (vv. 18-19).

IV. In Their Homes, the Midwives Received the Blessing of God (vv. 20-21).

CONCLUSION

These women are examples of how God reaches out to touch lives in the most unlikely places. The "fear of the LORD" was not reserved for the Hebrew women in this era of Jewish history, nor is it found only within "Christian" nations. God touched the lives of women even in the darkest and most unlikely places. The question is: Are you willing to receive Him into your life and obey Him? Will you stand for Him even in the most challenging and difficult situations?

Puah and Shiphrah were professional women doing a job. But they had sanctified that job with a fear of the Lord and respect for the Creator God. Whether because of the maternity in their feminine nature or the respect for life emanating from their fear of the Lord—or perhaps both—they refused to let holding a politically correct position destroy or distort their personal convictions. They were righteous, and they did not stop with a façade of righteousness; they were determined to do right, whatever the cost!

QUOTATIONS

"Then the word of the LORD came to me [the prophet Jeremiah], saying: 'Before I formed you in the womb I knew you; Before you were born I sanctified you; I ordained you a prophet to the nations'"(Jer. 1:4-5).

"I deplore the horrible crime of child murder. No matter what the motive, love of ease or the desire to save from suffering the unborn innocent, the woman is awfully guilty who commits the deed. It will burden her conscience for life. It will burden her soul in death. But, Oh! Thrice guilty is he who drove her to the desperation, which impelled her to the crime." Susan B. Anthony, July 1869

"If we don't stand up for children, then we don't stand for much." Marian Wright Edelman, founder and president of the Children's Defense Fund

"Abortion is the ultimate exploitation of women." Alice Paul, one of the leading figures responsible for the passage of the Nineteenth Amendment (women's suffrage) to the U.S. Constitution

"Courage is the most important of all the virtues, because without courage you can't practice any other virtue consistently. You can practice any virtue erratically, but nothing consistently without courage." Maya Angelou

"God's interest in the human race is nowhere better evinced than in obstetrics." Martin H. Fischer

MIDWIFERY

Pregnant women still choose to use midwives to assist in childbirth. In my home city of Fort Worth, two hospitals provide certification for these women who have training and experience to assist in this process. As a rule, they facilitate the birth without fuss or show. The mother is helped as needed, but she remains in charge to the extent she wants to be. They are thorough in using their professional skills but caring in treating their patients as family. The support of a midwife extends to the pregnancy and the post–partum period as well.

Midwives have delivered babies from the time of Moses, and their roles have evolved over the centuries of helping women have their babies in a natural way. In the modern era, these women work in birthing centers and hospitals in certified nurse-midwifery programs. Not only are midwives referenced in the Bible, but there was also a midwife on the *Mayflower*. At the birth of both Queen Victoria and Prince Albert from the British royal lineage, a midwife was in attendance. The word "midwife" in Old English means "with woman."

DOROTHY'S DICTUM

Find the principle in Scripture that speaks to the issue at hand. Be willing to respond in obedience whatever the cost. Call upon the Lord to guide and sustain you in the journey.

INDUCTIVE QUESTIONS

1. Describe a situation in which you were compelled to make a risky choice because you "feared God" (as in v. 17). If you have not had such an experience, find an example from the life of someone else.

2. In what way(s) are you demonstrating a personal pro-life stance in your community or sphere of influence?

3. God rewarded the midwives by giving them families. Though God does not always reward women who fear Him in this way, the verse does affirm God's perspective on families as a good gift. How has God demonstrated His goodness to you through your own family?

4. Examine your heart to identify any attitudes toward children that do not reflect those of God as revealed in Scripture.

    •   Do you really care about children other than your own? Or, do you care only about your child's rights, opportunities, performance, or safety?

    •   Could you list the needs of the poorest, most neglected child in your neighborhood, school, or church? Are you willing to find ways to meet any of his needs?

- Do you consistently choose not to get involved in situations or ministries in which your participation could extend God's love to a child? Is this personal cost too much for you?

SCARLET THREAD OF REDEMPTION

The midwives feared God, which is the beginning of wisdom. They did what they could to preserve life. God rewarded their obedience by giving them families.

MIRIAM: THE SISTER WHO SHADOWED HIM

Miriam, whose ancestry came through what became the priestly line of Levi, lived in Egypt, perhaps in the Nile River Valley in the general area of present-day Cairo. Her character was molded within a family setting in which faith in the God of Israel was a daily reality. Her godly parents bore and nurtured three great leaders—Moses, Aaron, and Miriam.

Miriam's name could be an amalgam of two Hebrew words—*mar*, meaning "bitter," and *yam*, meaning "sea." Some suggest that her name seemed to prophesy her future as one marked by "bitterness" or "rebellion."

Though Josephus, the first-century Jewish historian, suggested that Miriam married the Israelite judge Hur, the text of Scripture does not give any indication that Miriam ever married. In fact, she is portrayed as a single woman in a day when female celibacy was not the norm. Yet Miriam was called by God to an exceptional task and was greatly used of God as have been many other single women throughout history. Without responsibilities to husband and children, she was able to dedicate herself wholly to the kingdom ministry task God had given to her.

Miriam was proud of her heritage as an Israelite; she was a committed patriot. As an unnamed young girl (perhaps seven to ten years of age), she became a part of history in the biblical record. She was identified as the daughter of Jochebed and sister of Moses and Aaron. She was assigned the task of babysitting her youngest brother under the most adverse and dangerous circumstances (Exod. 2:4, 7).

Even in her early childhood, Miriam performed this duty with the poise, finesse, intelligence, and self-confidence that would characterize her bold leadership of the women of Israel. If the basket bearing her baby brother had been left on the river to float aimlessly, the death of the child would have only been postponed. Even if the basket had merely been rescued by the princess, the life of the child would have been saved, but his destiny might not have been fulfilled. Miriam was the key person to oversee the course of the floating cradle and then to intercede at just the right moment with a suggestion that not only ensured the baby's life but also helped to prepare him for his destiny.

MIRIAM'S RISK

In her assignment on the river bank, Miriam's boldness to step forward and address the daughter of Pharaoh was accompanied by an aloof discretion that included the absence of any tone or facial expression to betray her relationship to the baby boy. She acted with discernment, wisdom, and resourcefulness. After all, she sought to save the life of Moses; and furthermore, she seemed to sense her role in finding a way to be certain that Moses would be trained for the future. Although Miriam did not know God's ultimate plan for her brother, she may well have had some premonition that he would need to have an understanding of his Hebrew roots.

Miriam said nothing about the baby's birth heritage but casually suggested her availability to find a wet nurse for the crying infant. Miriam succeeded in arranging the employment of her mother as nurse to her own child, and divine providence opened the door for the baby to spend these earliest years in his birth home, nurtured by his own mother in the midst of a loving and God-honoring family circle.

Miriam was the catalyst for connecting two strategically important women who would preserve the life of Moses. Jochebed, the natural mother, would feed Moses and bind him to his birth heritage; the daughter of Pharaoh, his adoptive mother, would rear him to adulthood and prepare him for a place in the world. Miriam's connection of these two women was a precipitous event, but she had learned from her courageous mother how to take calculated risks under the direction of divine providence.

Women are often connected to preserve the lives and properties of their families, to serve their communities and country, and to further the purposes of God Himself. Consider Ruth and Naomi, Mary and Elizabeth. Their common needs and shared goals brought them together to do what neither could do alone. So it was with the lives of Jochebed and Miriam, the mother and daughter duo, who joined hands to become God's channel to save the life of Moses. Miriam had already learned from the example of her mother some noteworthy traits of character—commitment to the task at hand, resourcefulness, and creativity.

MIRIAM'S ABSENCE

Once Moses was weaned and returned to the household of Pharaoh and even when he was in exile in Midian, there is no record of Miriam. She is also absent from the record of the extended confrontations Moses and Aaron had with Pharaoh. Yet her absence from the pages of historical record does not for a moment suggest that she was silent and inactive. For her to take the leadership role she assumed among the women during the exodus, she must have already made her place in the hearts of the Hebrew people. Miriam must have been ministering and encouraging the people behind the scenes. She may well have been helping her brothers more by keeping the spirit of the people up during those days of uncertainty and waiting (Micah 6:4).

Miriam again appears on the pages of history as Israel's deliverance is at hand. The text implies that she had hardly seen Moses in the eighty years during which he had been in the household of Pharaoh and then in exile. She accepted the challenging position of leading the Israelite women, who would find themselves at the heart and center of all God planned to do with His people. Although most women in

Miriam's generation gave their first and primary energies to being wives and mothers, Miriam appears to have taken another path. She seems to have chosen to use her time, energies, and gifts in the public arena rather than in her home. Some would describe her as a politician or stateswoman, and every indication is that she was called of God to this task of leading the women of Israel.

THE PROPHETESS AND POET

Moses composed a song praising God and thanking Him for His kindness in delivering Israel from her oppressors. After Moses had concluded his song of victory and joy as the Israelites were delivered from their oppressive enemies, Miriam used her skills as a musician and poet to lead the Israelite women in song and dance.

With tambourine in hand, Miriam, who was well past middle age, led the women in chanting a brief verse of exultation from that song. This is now recognized as one of the earliest songs in all of Hebrew hymnody and one of their finest national anthems of praise. This song of victory bore testimony of the Lord: "You have triumphed!" (Exod. 15:21). Miriam's one verse, directly quoted from her brother's song, is brief; but even today it stirs the hearts of Jewish and Gentile women, inspiring them to write new songs, poems, and stories with their creative minds and ready pens.

The Bible describes Miriam as "the prophetess, Aaron's sister" (Exod. 15:20). In a general sense, prophets and prophetesses in Scripture are commissioned by God to speak His Word before the people. Miriam later declared that God had spoken through her, but no specific prophecies were recorded in Scripture (Num. 12:2). Perhaps this prophetic role helped to make her the most honored and renowned woman in Israel. She definitely played a God-appointed role in founding the nation of Israel and leading its people to their homeland.

Miriam was a strong woman to whom leadership came easily and naturally. But, as is often the case, this very strength became her greatest weakness. Miriam is not the only sister in the annals of history to be overshadowed by a younger brother and annoyed by his success. However, most sibling rivalry is not aired in so public a setting, nor does it produce such severe consequences. Moses' preeminence over his sister Miriam and his brother Aaron is unquestioned. This more prominent and powerful position of Moses seemingly awakened jealousy and bitterness in Miriam's heart over her secondary position; and she even enlisted the support of Aaron in airing her grievances (Num. 12:2).

Interestingly, most of us can point across the generations to similarities between our own respective lives and those who have gone before. For example, I am almost a decade older than my only brother. I, as Miriam, had the opportunity to babysit with him and hover over him as he grew into manhood. I, too, in some ways have been thrust into the public forum with speaking to groups of women around the world and writing for publication. In fact, perhaps I had name recognition before my brother came into his prime ministry. However, I learned very early that God had His hand on Chuck Kelley. He was anointed to preach the gospel, and his giftedness indicated early that he might be tapped for extraordinary service in the kingdom. Indeed, he is now president of a seminary just as my husband serves as president of a seminary. These two seminary presidents may compete for students, but the hearts of our entire family are knit together with a determination to serve the Lord. I am proud of both my husband and my brother; I am pleased to be "the wife of" and "the sister of," and these roles in themselves are worthy of my devotion and energies.

AMBITION

Miriam's blind ambition caused her to overestimate herself and drove her to seek greater prominence, even if in the process she had to discredit the leadership of her brother Moses. Miriam knew she was able, and she was proud of it. This ambition for greater political power blocked any genuine humility and contentment. She put herself in direct opposition to a servant of God anointed for his position of leadership. Whatever her purported concerns for her nation, she dismissed her concern for the well-being of her people or for her brother by her actions, which endangered the unity and future of the entire nation.

Despite her good name and worthy testimony, this one tragic blot on Miriam's life and ministry is preserved for the generations to come. How sad that one sinful act of rebellion can overshadow a life of service and mar a good name, for one fault often tends to blot out a multitude of virtues.

Miriam is joined by Aaron in criticizing their brother Moses concerning his marriage to a Cushite woman, a foreigner to the Israelites. This dark-skinned woman probably came from Ethiopia, an African country bordering Egypt. She may have accompanied the Israelites as they escaped from Egypt. Interestingly, the text offers no evidence that either Miriam or Aaron had raised any question about Moses' marriage to Zipporah, who as a Midianite was also a "foreign" wife.

Perhaps Miriam was incensed over the thought of a foreign woman being honored and thereby taking a position over her, a daughter of Israel, as the "First Lady" of Israel. In any case, even if Moses had erred in his marriage to the Cushite woman, the mistake would have been a personal one and not a public or corporate misdeed. The matter should have been between Moses and God and not an issue to be decided between Moses and his sister.

 Miriam could have made a wonderful contribution to her people as well as to her brother Moses if she had given Moses her wholehearted support in the super-human task that was his. She was already greatly honored as a prophetess; she was a leader over all the women of Israel. Aaron, too, was held in high esteem since he was the High Priest or spiritual leader of the whole nation. Yet both Miriam and Aaron disputed the preeminence of Moses and his exclusive position assigned by God Himself. They reacted by being proud of and boasting of their gifts instead of by being humble and exhibiting the modesty and gratitude they should have felt. Miriam was the instigator of the public rebellion, but Aaron willingly followed her.

The mistake of Miriam and Aaron was not so much because of the subject matter of their quarrel with Moses but the fact that they were speaking negatively, and in a public setting, about God's appointed leader. Those who are determined to speak unfairly about others, including divinely appointed leaders, do not seem to be inhibited by the fact that God hears every conversation.

PUNISHMENT

Miriam and Aaron were called forth to hear from God Himself what set Moses apart from other prophets (Num.12:6-8). God called for a private meeting with Moses and his siblings at the Tent of Meeting, in which the Lord appeared in a cloud. Yahweh, the God of Israel, did set the record straight in no uncertain terms. After His explanation, God departed, and immediately judgment fell. Miriam was stricken with leprosy—a horrible, contagious, disfiguring skin disease and in that day incurable. Affliction with this dreadful disease meant her immediate dismissal from the camp and exclusion from any association with others. Her brothers promptly interceded to the Lord on her behalf. Despite the animosity Miriam had shown toward him, Moses displayed a spirit of loving forgiveness toward his sister.

Some question why the punishment fell only on Miriam and not on Aaron, since both spoke against Moses. Aaron did stand with Miriam, but he was more or less a passive partner in the rebellion, and he did not seem to share her envy and bitterness. The biblical text is actually clear in suggesting that Miriam was indeed the primary offender (Num. 12:10). Not only is her name mentioned first, but the Hebrew verb used to describe their complaints in the biblical account is also the feminine singular. Aaron, too, was guilty, but the Bible clearly identifies Miriam as the instigator in this rebellion. After all, Aaron never did exhibit much of a mind of his own. He had already proven himself easy prey to be caught up and swept away—first by an idolatrous and rebellious people (Exod. 32) and then by an envious and jealous sister. Miriam was a leader who had come to overestimate herself and her importance! She had moved from God's control of her life to self-control, and that was not a wise move.

This harsh punishment of Miriam made it necessary for her to be shut out of the Israelite camp for a week even if the healing of her skin disorder happened immediately (Num. 12:14). The public punishment sent a message to the entire nation that God would punish those who thought too highly of themselves. It also served as a reminder that God reserves for Himself the appointment of His leaders and that He reserved that leadership for those who are humble enough to follow His pattern for servant leadership. She had sought to exclude the Cushite woman but then suffered the pain and humiliation of exclusion herself. The shortness of her stint as a leper showed clearly the abundant mercies of God and allowed Moses, through his quick and complete forgiveness, to show again the strength of character that made him a worthy vessel for leadership (Num. 12:3).

Aaron suffered his own punishment as he had to exercise the responsibility of his office of High Priest toward his sister by pronouncing her unclean because of the leprosy. He then forced her out of the camp and shut its gates behind her. He had to execute judgment on his own sister, with whom he had conspired in the sinful rebellion. When Moses wrote down the law concerning lepers and how they were to be treated, he used his sister Miriam as an example (Deut. 24:9).

PARADOX IN PUNISHMENT

There is a paradox in the punishment: Even prominent leaders and the "fairer sex" must experience punishment; on the other hand, respect for Miriam's leadership in the camp through the years and perhaps sensitivity toward Miriam as a woman tempered the response of Israel to her plight. The Israelite camp remained in place for the seven days of her confinement. Even though the people must have been weary of their long years in the wilderness and impatient to get on their way to the Promised Land, they did not continue their march until Miriam could join them (Num. 12:15).

Did Miriam learn from this tragedy? She was cured from the dread disease and reunited with her people. She received the forgiveness of her brother Moses, and perhaps even of her sister-in-law, the Cushite wife of Moses. Forgiven and restored, Miriam's bitterness was undoubtedly changed to sweetness and her rebellion to submission, but this sinful act left its ugly scar. Not only were the Hebrews slowed down in their march to the Promised Land, but her leadership and influence would never be the same.

HER FINAL DAYS

Miriam didn't reach the Promised Land. This beloved and forceful woman died in the wilderness at Kadesh, about seventy miles south of Hebron. Some suggest that she must have died of a broken heart. Certainly after this tragedy, she was a broken woman who never again regained her place of influence and honor among her people. Israel did mourn the passing of this outstanding leader. She was given a state funeral and buried on an unnamed mountain. Tradition identifies her burial place, like that of Aaron, who died in the same year, as being near Petra in modern-day Jordan. The people mourned for Miriam for thirty days. They did not continue their journey until the days of mourning and subsequent purification were complete (Num. 20:1).

Miriam appears to be a woman who took matters into her own hands. She was a self-starter; a doer, not merely a hearer or thinker. When this aggressiveness was harnessed by divine direction, she accomplished great things for God and country. Her quick thinking, ingenuity, and persever-ance saved the life of her brother and paved the way for na-tional deliverance. However, Miriam later made some wrong choices that precipitated serious consequences. When she chose to turn against her brother Moses, wielding her own personal power, she paid a tragic price—the breaking of fellowship with her brother, the marring of her relationship to YAHWEH, the loss of her own influence with the people.

As a prophetess and leader of women, she had been a powerful and influential woman, but her ambition and bitterness cost her that position of leadership and influence and very nearly cost her life. It was as if this self-absorbed woman, in seeking to put herself at the center of everything and over everyone and in determining to think exclusively about what she wanted, was erasing her opportunity for productive ministry. She had known what it was like to do a job without the appreciation she deemed appropriate, and that seemingly became too much for her.

PRAYER

Lord God, take my life and let it be used of You. Let my thoughts come from You; let my words flow from You; let my deeds emanate from Your heart. Let me be content with the position you assign to me. Let me rejoice in the service of others, especially of those near and dear to me. I thank you for the godly men in my life—a father who set my eyes on You; a brother who now serves You in a strategic kingdom position; a husband whose godly influence has been extended far beyond what either of us expected; sons who have already picked up the mantle of servant leadership. These men make me proud; I love them Lord. Help me be content with where you have placed me.

FURTHER STUDY

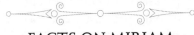

FACTS ON MIRIAM

- *Name:* Miriam
- *Scripture References:* Exodus 2:4-8; 15:20-21;
  Numbers 11:1-6; 12:1-15; 20:1; 26:59; Deuteronomy
  24:8-9; 1 Chronicles 6:3; 5:29; Micah 6:4
- *Family:* Daughter of Amram and Jochebed (Num. 26:59;
  1 Chron. 6:3); sister of Aaron and Moses
- *Marital Status:* Single (Josephus suggests she was the wife
  of Hur, an Israelite judge, but this is not in Scripture)
- *Occupation:* Leader of Israelite women (Exod. 15:1-21);
  prophetess
- *Spiritual Gifts:* Prophecy, exhortation, leadership
- *Dominant Characteristics:* Intelligent, courageous,
  resourceful, quick-witted, patriotic; an original thinker
- *Dates:*   Birth - *c.*1535 BC
            Ministry high point - 1445 BC
            Death - *c.*1407 BC

EXEGETICAL NOTES

Exodus 2:4, 7 "his sister"

The phrase identifies the relationship between Miriam and
Moses. Though the text does not state her age, the descrip-
tion of Miriam's actions in the text seem to suggest that she
was at least eight to ten years old but not yet a teenager.

Exodus 2:6 "felt sorry for him"

Perhaps due to her maternal instincts, Pharaoh's daughter felt
"sorry" (Hb. *chamal*, "pitied, had compassion") for the baby
in the basket and rescued him rather than leaving him to die.

Exodus 2:7 "a woman from the Hebrews to nurse the boy"

Miriam's offer to "call a nurse "was a sign of her resourcefulness and sensitivity to divine guidance. Her question may

have come according to the careful instruction of her mother; but surely in the pressures of the moment and genius of the plan, her response was prompted by God Himself. It was done at exactly the right moment with precisely the right words and was rewarded by divine providence in a way too wonderful to have been anticipated.

Exodus 15:20 "Miriam the prophetess"

"Prophetess" (Hb. *nevi'ah*, the feminine form of *navi'*, "prophet, spokesman") is used to describe Miriam's leadership of the Israelite women as they celebrated what the Lord had done.

Numbers 12:1 "the Cushite woman he remarried"

"The Cushite woman" is probably a reference to Moses' wife Zipporah (cf. Exod. 2:21; 4:25) but could have been a woman he married after Zipporah's death since she was not mentioned after Exodus 18. Cush was located south of Egypt.

Numbers 12:3 "a very humble man"

Moses is described as "humble," affirming that he did not act with arrogance, flaunting his God-given authority.

Numbers 12:8 "I speak with him directly"

The expression "speak with him face to face" (Hb. *peh-el peh*, literally "mouth to mouth") clearly affirms the intimate fellowship Moses enjoyed with the Lord.

Numbers 12:9 "the Lord's anger burned against them"

The Lord's disposition toward Miriam and Aaron for their affront to Moses' leadership was "anger" (Hb. *'aph*). This Hebrew word literally refers to the "nostrils" but metaphorically denotes "anger," which is often shown by hard breathing, and/or flared nostrils. Similarly you might describe an angry person as "huffing and puffing" or "blowing off steam." "The anger of the Lord" is always a righteous response to sin and usually results in punishment or destruction (cf. Num. 11:1, 10; 25:3-4; Deut. 6:14-15).

Numbers 12:14 "spit in her face"

The Lord compared Miriam's shame to having her father spit in her face, which would have been the ultimate shame in the ancient Near East.

68

PARALLEL REFERENCES

Exodus 15:20-21

Then Miriam the prophetess, the sister of Aaron, took the timbrel in her hand; and all the women went out after her with timbrels and with dances. And Miriam answered them:

"Sing to the LORD,
For He has triumphed gloriously!
The horse and its rider
He has thrown into the sea!"

Numbers 12:1-16

Then Miriam and Aaron spoke against Moses because of the Ethiopian woman whom he had married; for he had married an Ethiopian woman. So they said, "Has the LORD indeed spoken only through Moses? Has He not spoken through us also?" And the LORD heard *it*. (Now the man Moses *was* very humble, more than all men who *were* on the face of the earth.) Suddenly the LORD said to Moses, Aaron, and Miriam, "Come out, you three, to the tabernacle of meeting!" So the three came out. Then the LORD came down in the pillar of cloud and stood *in* the door of the tabernacle, and called Aaron and Miriam. And they both went forward. Then He said,

"Hear now My words:
If there is a prophet among you,
I, the LORD, make Myself known to him in a vision;
I speak to him in a dream.

Not so with My servant Moses;
He *is* faithful in all My house.

I speak with him face to face,
Even plainly, and not in dark sayings;
And he sees the form of the LORD.
Why then were you not afraid
to speak against My servant Moses?"

So the anger of the LORD was aroused against them, and He departed. And when the cloud departed from above the tabernacle, suddenly Miriam *became* leprous, as *white as* snow. Then Aaron turned toward Miriam, and there she was, a leper. So Aaron said to Moses, "Oh, my lord! Please do not lay *this* sin on us, in which we have done foolishly and in which we have sinned. Please do not let her be as one dead, whose flesh is half consumed when he comes out of his mother's womb!"

So Moses cried out to the LORD, saying, "Please heal her, O God, I pray!" Then the LORD said to Moses, "If her father had but spit in her face, would she not be shamed seven days? Let her be shut out of the camp seven days, and afterward she may be received again." So Miriam was shut out of the camp seven days, and the people did not journey till Miriam was brought in again. And afterward the people moved from Hazeroth and camped in the Wilderness of Paran.

Deuteronomy 24:8-9

Take heed in an outbreak of leprosy, that you carefully observe and do according to all that the priests, the Levites, shall teach you; just as I commanded them, so you shall be careful to do. Remember what the LORD your God did to Miriam on the way when you came out of Egypt!

1 Chronicles 6:1

The sons of Levi were Gershon, Kohath, and Merari.

1 Chronicles 6:2-3

The Sons of Kohath were Amram, Izhar, Hebron, and Uzziel. The children of Amram were Aaron, Moses, and Miriam. And the sons of Aaron were Nadab, Abihu, Eleazar, and Ithamar.

Micah 6:4

For I brought you up from the land of Egypt, I redeemed you from the house of bondage; And I sent before you Moses, Aaron, and Miriam.

TEACHING OUTLINE

INTRODUCTION

Miriam demonstrated early her keen mind and tender heart when she first appeared beside the Nile River in her role of protecting her baby brother Moses. After successfully overseeing his journey to safety, Miriam disappeared for eighty years with no record of her role among the people of Israel until after their exodus from Egypt.

As the Hebrews moved forward toward the Promised Land, Miriam assumed her role as leader of the women. For forty years, she had been sister, perhaps surrogate mother, and closest female companion and friend to her brother Moses. Her gifts as prophetess, poet, and musician gave her a place of influence alongside her brothers Moses and Aaron.

However, Miriam's ambition, pride, and envy caused her publicly to reject the leadership of Moses. She was stricken with leprosy as a result and expelled from the camp. In response to the prayers of her brothers, Miriam was healed and later allowed to reenter the camp. Yet there is no evidence that her influence was ever again blessed of God, and she died before reaching the Promised Land (Num. 20:1).

I.   Faithful in Preparing for Leadership (Exod. 2:1-10)
    A. A Godly Family Heritage (vv. 1-4)
    B. An Alert and Sensitive Attitude (vv. 5-8)
    C. Creative and Resourceful Actions (vv. 9-10)

II.   Joy in Serving the Lord (Exod. 15:20-21)
    A. Recognizing an Opportunity (v. 20)
    B. Doing the Task (v. 21)

III.   The Tragedy of Jealousy and Bitterness (Num. 12:1-12)
    A. The Danger of Rejecting God-Appointed Authorities (vv. 1-3)
    B. The Accountability for Wrong Choices (vv. 4-8)
    C. The Consequences of Disobedience (vv. 9-12)

IV.   The Mercy of Forgiveness (Num. 12:13-16)
    A. The Intercession of a Servant Leader, i.e., Moses (vv. 14-15)
    B. The Punishment for Disobedience, Tempered by Divine Mercy (v. 16)

CONCLUSION

God alone bestows giftedness, and He calls out and assigns leadership according to His sovereign purposes. When Miriam challenged the authority of Moses at Hazeroth (Num. 12:1-15), she also questioned the authority of God Himself. Her jealousy, insubordination, and bitterness robbed her of a good ending. Yet Miriam does leave a legacy. She had a song in the wilderness; she offered hope for women who were hurting and broken and exhausted. You, too, need a song in your wilderness. Women who can bring encouragement and praise even in those desert moments of life are needed.

QUOTATIONS

"All of us, not just we strong-willed women, are naturally defiant toward God before his spirit draws us to himself and we are radically changed. We strong-willed women just have a different sin-pattern with which to deal: that of trying to control not only our lives but those of our families, colleagues, and friends. Running to Jesus in repentance is an everyday necessity so that we can love and forgive others in the way Jesus loves and forgives us. - Sharon Hall." Quoted by Cynthia Ulrich Tobias in *Redefining the Strong-willed Woman: How to Effectively Use Your Strong Will for God* (Grand Rapids: Zondervan, 2002), 132.

"Every time you make a choice you are turning the central part of you, the part of you that chooses, into something a little different from what it was before ... either into a creature that is in harmony with God...or into one that is in a state of war with God. Each of us at each moment is progressing to the one state or the other."C. S. Lewis, *Mere Christianity* (New York: HarperCollins, 1980), 92.

DOROTHY'S DICTUM

Refuse the bitter root of jealousy prompted by personal pride. Embrace the gift of the Lord's presence as the "God of all comfort" in your life.

INDUCTIVE QUESTIONS

1. Identify a Christian woman who actively serves the Lord in an exemplary way. Interview her to learn more about her priorities and activities. Encourage her in her leadership role.

2. Evaluate your own interests and gifts and list ways you can draw women to Christ and teach Christian life disciplines.

3. Write two lists. These lists should cover how you should and should not deal with issues or complaints about a Christian ministry. Include Scripture references or biblical examples supporting these guidelines.

4. In Numbers 12:2, Miriam and Aaron asked, "Has the Lord spoken only through Moses?" and "Hasn't he [the Lord] also spoken through us?" What similar questions have you asked, whether in your heart as you struggled with jealousy or in a conversation discussing the faults or mistakes of someone in leadership?

SCARLET THREAD OF REDEMPTION

Miriam is the recipient of the faithful love and everlasting mercies of the Lord: She was given an extraordinary opportunity for service to her family, nation, and the Lord.

Miriam did many of the divinely appointed tasks assigned to her well. She ultimately allowed her own pride and jealousy of her brother to destroy her ministry and usefulness. In the end, her brother Moses forgave her offense against him, and the Lord brought her back into the camp and under the wings of His protection; but her public ministry was ended prematurely. Anyone redeemed by the Lord is secure, but how tragic to lose the opportunity for significant service.

PHARAOH'S DAUGHTER: THE WOMAN WHO REARED HIM

Amazingly you are all players in the drama of the providence of God. You find yourself seizing opportunities without realizing they are God-assigned. Pharaoh's daughter had no idea of the impact her actions would eventually make on her own world. She must have carried her secret well, for she reared a Hebrew son as her own. In the divine economy, when God gets ready to rescue His enslaved people, He can bring nations to their knees. In the case of delivering Israel from Egypt, God used an unlikely group of women to instigate and execute the whole plan.

In ancient Egypt, women in the royal household derived their importance from their relationship to the pharaoh. Egyptian tradition presents the pharaoh as divine and set apart from other human beings, which, in essence, would suggest that the nation had been ruled by successive male gods—or at the very least by human beings who were possessed of some measure of divinity—from the time of creation. Within the pharaoh's immediate circle were a number of royal women, including his mother, his wives, and his daughters.

Interestingly, for centuries Egyptologists have reiterated the belief that the throne of Egypt was transmitted through the female line of the royal family. Although this right to the throne passed through the female line, the office of pharaoh was not exercised by the royal woman herself but through the man she married. For that reason, a man who wanted to be pharaoh would consolidate his right to the throne by marrying his sister or half-sister. By marrying his sister, the pharaoh would be setting himself apart from his subjects, who did not normally marry their sisters; and he also considered this pattern as a way of imitating the gods and making the bloodline more pure, thus stressing the divine nature of the pharaoh. It would also stand to reason that a wife who was equally descended from the founders of the dynasty would have the same interests vested in the familial dynasty, bringing her own intelligence and political intuitions to her husband and thus to the throne.

HER IDENTITY

Josephus identified this daughter of Pharaoh as Thermuthis, but some evangelical scholars suggest that the famous Hatchepsut was the surrogate mother of Moses.[1] Her life span does fit the dating suggested by many Old Testament scholars who favor an early date for the exodus.

Hatchepsut was the only surviving child of Thutmose I and Ahmose. She would actually have ascended to the throne as pharaoh if women had been allowed to rule since she was the only descendant of the old Theban princes who had fought and expelled the foreign Hyksos rulers. Thutmose I ruled only by virtue of his marriage to Ahmose. He was evidently a large man, with bull-like strength and singleness of purpose, who completed the expulsion of the Hyksos people. He was immensely popular with the common people of Egypt. Since Thutmose I and Ahmose produced no male heirs, Thutmose II, the son of one of Thutmose's lesser wives, ascended the throne. He married Hatchepsut (who would have been the more legitimate successor to Pharaoh, except for her gender), his stepsister, to consolidate his power. Hatchepsut was willing to share bed and throne with this weak man in order to fulfill her own dreams and destiny.

---

[1] Walter C. Kaiser, Jr., "Exodus," in *The Expositor's Bible Commentary*, vol. 2, ed. Frank E. Gaebelein (Grand Rapids: Zondervan, 1990), n.5, 310.

Thutmose II was sickly even at his coronation, making it easy for Hatchepsut to dominate the court and establish her own power base. Upon the death of Thutmose II, Hatchepsut easily increased her power as regent for her young stepson Thutmose III since he acquired his right to rule through her legitimacy. Historians later described Thutmose III as the greatest pharaoh ever to occupy the throne of Egypt.

This influence of the royal women should be acknowledged and respected. In any generation, wives, as true partners to their husbands, play an important part in the functioning of their families and in the responsibilities of their husbands.

The Theban royal family seemed to allow its queens to have a more prominent role in government, but there is no evidence that the queen ever took precedence over the all-powerful pharaoh. Even Hatchepsut, who seemed to be an exception to this rule, assumed the powers of the pharaoh only after she had transformed herself into the pharaoh, including portraying herself as a man by wearing a false beard and dressing as a man.

Interestingly, even in matrilineal systems, in which descent is traced through the female rather than the male line, the proof of a female-dominated state, although popular with feminist historians, has not been substantiated. It certainly was not the case in Egypt.

The close-knit Theban royal family, of which Hatchepsut was a member, had struggled to unite Egypt at the end of the period that straddled the artificial division between the seventeenth and eighteenth dynasties of Egypt. The family was marked by fierce militarism; by promoting the new state god Amen; by architectural, artistic, and technological advances; and by its liberal treatment of royal women. Hatchepsut herself had a strong personality and possessed a remarkable gift for leadership.

Concerning Hatchepsut and her tenure in the royal household, there are huge gaps in the historical records and little other than the monuments to testify of her achievements. Even contemporary records of this period are most often documents, which, because of their official nature, rarely expressed any private opinions. In fact, there is not even concrete information on Hatchepsut's physical appearance since her representations in the monuments and all formal portraits were designed to depict her as the ideal divine Egyptian pharaoh and thus as a man. Once Hatchepsut adopted the throne of Pharaoh, on the monuments dedicated to her, if not in her everyday life, she appeared in the male costume of a pharaoh.

Hatchepsut was not only the daughter of Pharaoh Thutmose I and thus a princess of the royal blood, but she was also queen consort to Thutmose II, who was not compelled by law of tradition to take his sister as his chief wife but chose to do so for his own reasons. From the historical records that do exist, Hatchepsut seemed to pay due honor to her husband as a traditional wife and later served respectfully as queen regent, according all the honor due a fellow monarch to her stepson Thutmose III, the son of one of her husband's minor wives. She arranged a marriage between Thutmose III and her daughter Neferure.

Although Hatchepsut must have understood that she was meant to hand over control of the kingdom to her stepson when he was old enough to rule for himself, she likely did not look upon that prospect with any joy. She made use of the institution of co-regency, having herself crowned "king" or "pharaoh" without actually removing Thutmose III, her stepson, from the throne. Although she undoubtedly was the dominant partner in this rule, Thutmose III remained pharaoh throughout the reign of Hatchepsut. Hatchepsut is the only "usurper" to the Egyptian throne who was able to survive and tolerate the rightful heir to the throne by her side so that he assumed the throne upon her death.[2]

History reveals that Hatchepsut was a valid monarch. She had to go through carefully calculated political maneuvering to become accepted on the throne, but once recognized as

---

[2] Erika Feucht, "Women," in *The Egyptians*, ed. Sergio Donadoni (Chicago: University of Chicago Press, 1997), 341-42.

Pharaoh, she brought peace and prosperity to her nation. She devoted herself to building monuments rather than to wars of conquest as did her father Thutmose I and stepson Thutmose III. She is also the only queen who chose to represent herself as a man in her official depictions and inscriptions. Another queen, Elizabeth I of England, inherited her throne during a time of dynastic difficulty when there were no sons to ascend the throne. She, too, stressed her relationship to her royal and very effective father/monarch. Elizabeth I expressed her position in these words: "And though I be a woman, yet I have as good a courage, answerable to my place, as ever my father had."

HATCHEPSUT'S DEATH

Hatchepsut brought vast experience to the throne of Egypt and steered her country through peaceful and prosperous years, including ruling amicably alongside her young stepson. The assumption is that Hatchepsut died of natural causes, although some believe she was forcibly removed from the throne by her stepson.

In some ways, Hatchepsut looms larger in death than in life. In my humble opinion, there is no more spectacular burial monument in the world than her temple at Deir el-Bahri in Upper Egypt. You can still visit this spectacular edifice today. It was the first temple in Egypt to utilize terraces, allowing the construction at different levels and cutting the most sacred part of the temple into the mountain. The temple rises to three levels connected by central ramps. At the ends of the terraces are halls, within which she sought to make her reign legitimate in history by portraying herself as descending from the gods. In addition to scenes of her "divine" birth, she is presented as kneeling beneath the goddess Hathor, who is fashioned as a cow feeding Hatchepsut with her milk—a scene of "udder delight" still marked by artistic design and vivid colors! Other scenes depict Hatchepsut's coronation by the gods. This superb temple with its magnificent colonnades fits perfectly into its natural setting backed by the tremendous rocky fortress. The ivory white walls give the appearance of alabaster marble, and they are covered with exquisite art—figures and hieroglyphs in rich colors.

THE BIBLICAL ACCOUNT

In the biblical account, Pharaoh's daughter is a flesh-and-blood woman and not merely a one-dimensional character in history. She is portrayed in a favorable light, despite her connection to the wicked tyrant and enemy of Israel, the pharaoh with whom Moses interacted before the exodus.

The princess approached the Nile, probably to begin or continue her beauty ritual. Pharaoh had prescribed the Nile to be the means of death, but his daughter would have a part in reversing that tomb of death and destruction into a song of life and deliverance. Pharaoh's daughter became the agent for foiling her father's destructive plan. She probably sent her maidservant into the muddy waters of the Nile to fetch the basket out of curiosity. The maiden is unnamed; yet she, too, has a part in this redemptive drama. Women frequently are left out of the credit lines. Nevertheless, you as a woman are expected to be faithful to step out and do your part with no thought of "What's in it for me?"

When the princess saw the baby's face and the beauty of his countenance and heard his cry, she responded with sincerity and honor; she had pity and compassion on the infant and loved him enough to risk her own favorable position with the pharaoh. In order to save the baby's life, she determined to adopt the Hebrew boy as her own and provide for him the best education Egypt had to offer. The child became hers legally through some form of adoption.

Obviously the social and legal position of the woman in Egypt must have been relatively high and secure since the princess herself, without the assistance of any male figure from the royal household, negotiated and concluded the hiring of a wet nurse for the baby boy she had rescued. This status resulted in part from the matrilineal descent within the families of Egypt.

THE WET NURSE
The "wet nurse contract" provided payment to the woman hired for the service of suckling the infant in her own home. This was usually for a period of two to three years. Being chosen as a wet nurse for the royal household was an honor that benefited the woman and her family. She was held in high esteem and considered as an extended part of the family. She participated in the upbringing of the child and even carried the same title as male tutors. In Egyptian hieroglyphics this title was illustrated by a female breast.

The child would be returned to the palace after his weaning. In this case, the adoption would not take place until after the weaning, probably because of the very high infant mortality rate. If the baby died in the care of the wet nurse, there would be no need to go through the legal procedures involved in adoption.[3]

The Egyptian princess would never have agreed to using the baby's own mother as a wet nurse; but because Miriam skillfully intervened to provide what was needed by the princess in the way of child care, the detail of Jochebed's relationship to Moses was discreetly overlooked. As a result, Pharaoh's daughter got the very best for her new son—the nurturing of his own birth mother.

THE CHILD'S NAME
The princess named the baby "Moses," a name that most scholars agree is Egyptian in origin, deriving from the Egyptian *mses*, meaning "son of," as in Ramses, "son of Ra." She might have recognized the possibility of a parallel name in Hebrew when she added the explanation, "Because I drew him out of the water." However, the name could also represent a wordplay so that the princess bestowed on the child an Egyptian name, which has since been interpreted as a Hebrew word from a similar root, meaning "to draw out (from the water)," a word exceedingly rare in the biblical vocabulary.

---
[3] Feucht, *Women*, 329.

More than likely the princess gave the Hebrew child an Egyptian name, which the biblical writer has reinterpreted in terms of a Hebrew verb with the idea that Pharaoh's daughter had unknowingly rescued one who would deliver the Hebrew people from her father's oppression. In other words, the name prophesies the destiny of Moses. The phrase of interpretation could also merely be an inspired addition to prepare the reader for Moses' role as the one who would draw his people out of slavery. It would have been unusual for the princess to be familiar enough with Hebrew etymology to give such information on her own.

Although the Bible is silent on the years Moses spent in the palace of Pharaoh, it is obvious that he spent the formative years of his life in the royal court under the close supervision of his adoptive mother. An Egyptian mother traditionally did oversee the education of her children.

According to Egyptian tradition, Moses would have begun his education at the approximate age of four years, attending school from early in the morning until noonday for about twelve years. Discipline was undoubtedly exceedingly strict, according to an Egyptian proverb, "The ears of a boy are on his back; he hears when he is beaten."[4]

Although the curriculum centered on reading, writing, and arithmetic, the art of penmanship was also uniquely important to the Egyptians and a major prerequisite for an adequate education. Egyptian pedagogy seemed to emphasize drill and memorization.

From his foster family, Moses received knowledge and wisdom that would equip him to deal effectively with Pharaoh and his court when he would later seek the release of the Hebrews from Egypt. In other words, he had on-the-job training in court protocol and the means to have ready access to the royal court.

---

[4] Nahum M. Sarna, *Exploring Exodus*: *The Origins of Biblical Israel* (New York: Schocken Books, 1996), 33.

Hatchepsut, if indeed she is the daughter of Pharaoh referenced in this rescue of Moses, must have had a major role in this preparation. Historians do portray Thutmose III as a well-educated man of great energy, a fearless warrior and skilled horseman, even a composer of literary work. Seemingly his accomplishments would be a credit to the upbringing of his stepmother Hatchepsut. If this is the case, you could surmise that she also played a key role in the education of Moses.

Nevertheless, even the best education of Egypt would have left Moses unprepared for his future. In addition to the knowledge and skills he acquired in the royal court, Moses also must have bonded with his mother and birth family in a unique way during his first few years of life; for it was the values and beliefs and even ethnic ancestry of his birth parents that became the driving force in his life and work.

PRAYER

Lord God, you are all-powerful; you are sufficient to meet my needs in any challenge. Your providence is above and beyond human understanding. I pray that you will continue to move, even in pagan households of influence, to accomplish your purposes. What a mighty God I serve!

FURTHER STUDY

FACTS ON DAUGHTER OF PHARAOH

- *Name:* Unknown. However, in this volume, her identity is suggested as Hatchepsut (Hatasu, Hashepsowe, Hatshopsitu, Hapshepsut, Hatshepsut, and Hatshepsuit), who was the daughter of a pharaoh, the wife of a pharaoh, the stepmother of a pharaoh, and for a time a woman who actually acted as the pharaoh

- *Scripture References:* Exodus 2:5-10; Hebrews 11:23-26.

- *Family* (if Hatchepsut): Daughter of Thutmose I; chief wife of Thutmose II; stepmother of Thutmose III

- *Marital Status:* Not clearly stated in the Bible

- *Occupation:* Member of the royal household

- *Spiritual Gifts:* None

- *Dominant Characteristics:* Bold, curious, courageous, compassionate, headstrong, daring

- *Dates:* Reign of Hatchepsut 1504–1482 BC

  Death of Hatchepsut 1482 BC. Although there are a number of suggested time spans, this one is accepted by a number of Egyptologists.

EXEGETICAL NOTES

Exodus 2:5 "went down to bathe"

The expression "went down" was a natural way of noting access to the Nile. Because of annual flooding all housing and commercial areas, and especially the palace complex, were built on higher ground.

The princess may not have come to the river to "bathe" in the sense of a private beauty routine since the palace undoubtedly had the most luxurious bathing facilities.

Rather this routine trip to the banks of the Nile may suggest that this ritual was a sacred ablution since the pantheistic Egyptians considered the Nile a sacred treasure with health-giving effects and spiritual significance.

Exodus 2:6 "she saw the child – a little boy"
The words "child" (Hb. *na'ar*) and "baby" (Hb. *yeled*) refer to a male child without the ambiguity of the English translations, which can refer to a child of either sex. In this case the reader needs to be reminded of the sexual identity of the baby to emphasize that he was under an edict of death.

The identity of the baby boy as one of the Hebrew children was easily affirmed through the unique ethnic differences between Hebrews and Egyptians, clothing, and perhaps even the location of the discovery as near an Israelite community. There was also the common knowledge of the edict of death hanging over Hebrew, and not Egyptian, baby boys. In addition, a closer look would have revealed the covenant sign in the baby's flesh, i.e., circumcision.

Exodus 2:10 "he became her son"
The phrase "he became her son" is understood by all adoptive parents. Love seems to awaken when you see a child who needs the love and care you are in a position to give.

PARALLEL REFERENCES

Acts 7:20-22
At this time Moses was born, and was well pleasing to God; and he was brought up in his father's house for three months. But when he was set out, Pharaoh's daughter took him away and brought him up as her own son. And Moses was learned in all the wisdom of the Egyptians, and was mighty in words and deeds.

Hebrews 11:24
By faith Moses, when he became of age, refused to be called the son of Pharaoh's daughter.

TEACHING OUTLINE

INTRODUCTION

This daughter of Pharaoh must have been a daring and headstrong young woman. She was attracted to the infant floating on the Nile even when she discovered his Hebrew lineage. Yet she was strangely drawn to the baby, and her compassions were awakened.

In addition, she was an independent woman who knew what she wanted and proceeded to reach her goals. She promptly accepted Miriam's offer to secure a wet nurse from among the Hebrew women, set wages, and arranged for the care of the infant—all without consulting her father or anyone else. Surely such a capable Egyptian princess must have taken personal responsibility for overseeing the education of her foster son, being certain that he was schooled in the best of Egyptian wisdom as well as mentoring him in the responsibilities of court life and introducing him to the movers and shakers within the Egyptian government.

I. An Unexpected Opportunity for an Unsuspecting Woman (Exod. 2:5-16)
   A. The Framework of Mundane Routines (v. 5)
   B. The Adventure of Happenstance Events (v. 6)

II. A Response to Divine Providence by a Young Girl Assigned to Duty (Exod. 2:7-9)
   A. The Question Posed by an Israelite Girl (v. 7)
   B. The Response of an Egyptian Princess (v. 8)
   C. The God-inspired Solution for All (v. 9)

III. The Reward of Obedient Service and Divine Appointment (Exod. 2:10)
   A. The Saving of a Baby Boy
   B. The Gift of an Adopted Son
   C. The Deliverance of a Mother's Son

CONCLUSION

Perhaps this surrogate mother, as a princess of Egypt, even dreamed that Moses would one day become pharaoh. In any case, she must have done her work well. Moses grew into manhood with every advantage the royal household had to offer. This preparation was a key to equipping him to do the task to which God called him in later years.

QUOTATIONS

"However motherhood comes to you, it's a miracle." Valerie Harper, an adoptive parent.

"The first question which the priest and the Levite asked was: 'If I stop to help this man, what will happen to me?' But . . . the good Samaritan reversed the question: 'If I do not stop to help this man, what will happen to him?'" Martin Luther King, Jr.

"For as many as are led by the Spirit of God, these are sons of God. For you did not receive the spirit of bondage again to fear, but you received the Spirit of adoption by whom we cry out, 'Abba, Father.' The Spirit Himself bears witness with our spirit that we are children of God, and if children, then heirs—heirs of God and joint heirs with Christ, if indeed we suffer with Him, that we may also be glorified together"(Rom. 8:14-17).

DOROTHY'S DICTUM

Being at the right place at the right time is often the work of divine providence. The obedience that enables you to be part of a God-event is always your choice. In the end, you are rewarded with the satisfaction of service to the Lord, and the Lord is glorified and His name honored.

INDUCTIVE QUESTIONS

1. Recount a situation in which you recognize that God worked on your behalf through a non-Christian. Write down what took place and pray for an opportunity to tell someone how God acted on your behalf. If possible, share with the non-Christian what God has done and how you saw the Lord's work through that person. Perhaps this will prompt the unbeliever to consider the existence and sovereignty of God and to listen to the gospel.

2. Pharaoh's daughter not only "had compassion on" the crying baby but also acted on that compassion, boldly and decisively. What concrete action might the Lord be leading you to take in response to the compassion He has placed in your heart toward a child or children in hopeless circumstances?

3. Miriam's offer to find a Hebrew wet nurse may have been the catalyst for the decision of Pharaoh's daughter to make the baby her own, linking her natural tenderness for a crying baby with her ability to provide for his care. Identify possible ways for believers to encourage women of influence to invest their resources in ministries and agencies that promote adoption instead of abortion.

SCARLET THREAD OF REDEMPTION

Even though an Egyptian princess was used of God to deliver from premature death one of the greatest Hebrew deliverers in Jewish history, she did not receive salvation herself because she never acknowledged her own sinfulness, asked for forgiveness of her sins, and embraced Yahweh the God of Israel for herself.

ZIPPORAH: THE WOMAN
HE MARRIED

When Moses fled Egypt after committing a capital crime, he chose the mountains of Midian in northern Arabia, east of the Gulf of Aqabah, as his place of hiding. The tribe of Midian, sometimes called Kenites, are mentioned in the Old Testament and dwelt in this region (Num. 24:21). The name "Kenite" is not actually perceived to be an ethnic designation but rather is a reference to the occupation of metal-work. The Kenites were a nomadic clan who specialized in this craft of metalworking and who were associated with the Midianites during the period of Moses.

The Midianites originated from Abraham through his second wife Keturah, who bore a son named Midian (Gen. 25:1-2). These Midianites oppressed Israel in the days of the judges and even promoted the pagan worship of Baal in Israel (Judg. 6–8). Although Abraham surely loved all of his sons, including Ishmael, the son of his concubine, as well as the sons of Keturah, his second wife, the Bible is clear that neither Hagar nor Keturah were on the same level as Sarah, the mother of Isaac, who was the son of promise. This fact may account for the animosity that has plagued the land and people of the Middle East as Israel has continued to suffer at the hands of the descendants of Hagar and Keturah even to the present day.

Jethro (also known as Reuel, meaning "friend of God," and as Hobab) was the priest of Midian. He became the father-in-law of Moses as well as his advisor and counselor (Exod. 2:16; 3:1; 18:1-27). The use of different names has been addressed in a variety of ways. The names could involve several generations. For example, Reuel could have been a reference to the grandfather of Zipporah. The remaining two names can also be explained by seeing "Jethro" as an official priestly title rather than a personal name, with Hobab being the personal name. In any case, the confusion that may result from the use of various names assigned to Zipporah's father does not affect our look into her life.

As a descendant of Abraham, Jethro may have been a God-fearing man; and this connection, together with his own priestly function, could explain his affinity for Moses. The Bible does not record what god or gods Reuel served as priest, nor is there any discussion of his spiritual life. Moses seemed to develop an especially close relationship to his father-in-law. He obviously considered Jethro to be wise and discerning. Moses even accepted rather harsh criticism from Jethro and adopted the older man's solution to his problems in administering justice to the people.

THE LITTLE BIRD

Zipporah, whose name means "little bird,"[1] appears only briefly in the biblical text. Although a shepherdess, like Rachel, a revered heroine of Israel and wife of the biblical patriarch Jacob, Zipporah seems both impetuous and resistive. There is no evidence in the text that she appreciated her husband Moses, a leader greatly respected by his peers and honored by succeeding generations; nor did she express any interest in his religion or acknowledge any value in his work of leading the nation of Israel. The text gives no evidence that Zipporah considered her husband a hero in any way!

---

[1] Sometimes parents would use animal names for their children. Perhaps the name expresses a parental wish or challenge for the child, such as the name "Deborah" (meaning "bee"), suggesting the challenge for the daughter to become busy as a "bee." The name could suggest her lifestyle, as with "Rachel" (meaning "sheep"), who looked after her father's flocks. In this case, Zipporah, as an infant, may have been petite as a "bird."

However, before judging her too harshly, you must consider that Scripture does give evidence that she married a difficult man with complex needs, and he did incur overwhelming responsibilities, which most certainly would have added to his pressures and thus the stress that would fall upon those closest to him.

ZIPPORAH'S CHALLENGE

The challenge of a preoccupied and frequently absent husband is one that has often faced the wives of spiritual as well as government and business leaders. A man with heavy responsibilities and overwhelming demands on his time and energies from those outside the family circle may find it easy to block out his family while retreating from the world, assuming that those closest to him will understand his need for solitude and personal time. What a tragedy for him and them! For the greatest human comfort and solace is found in intimate fellowship and nurtured relationships.

Zipporah was obviously a woman acquainted with hard work and even physical labor. She, together with her sisters, had responsibility for their father's flocks. Zipporah's traveling was done on foot and could have included carrying sick or wounded sheep or goats back to the family tent from faraway fields. She was continually exposed to the elements of nature and other dangers.

Zipporah seemed detached from her own family. Before her marriage to Moses, she did not meet his family. He himself had not had any contact with his birth family for approximately eighty years. Zipporah was distrusted by the Israelites; she was hated by the Egyptians. If she did have a relationship with Yahweh God, it must have been fresh and unnurtured and is not mentioned in Scripture.

Zipporah's introduction to Moses came under circumstances that might be considered romantic by some. As Moses was fleeing from Egypt, he stopped at a well for water. There Zipporah and her six sisters came to water the flock of their father. Some ruffian shepherds had also stopped at the well, as was their habit, to harass and mock the girls and attempt to drive them away. Moses again became caught up in someone else's battle. He rescued the girls, helped them water the flock, and in the process discouraged the rude shepherds. Moses was continuing in the path he had set for himself of fighting injustice, and this time he was not fighting for his own people but for members of a tribe who had formerly allied themselves against his people.

When Reuel learned of this timely rescue by an "Egyptian," he sent the girls to invite their deliverer to dinner. Because Moses had been reared in the household of Pharaoh and was educated in the history and culture of Egypt, he must have looked and dressed and talked like an Egyptian. One thing led to another, and soon a betrothal was in progress. Moses remained in the household of Reuel and married his daughter Zipporah.

Whether or not Reuel and his family knew the Hebrew ancestry of Moses at the time of the wedding is not mentioned in the biblical text. From the text, there is no evidence that Zipporah shared the same spiritual disciplines as Moses. Perhaps Moses agreed to compromise on the matter of circumcision to keep peace with his wife, or he may have become lax in his own commitments to the Lord as he found himself in another arena of life. Nevertheless, his Hebrew roots did become apparent in a later incident when Yahweh God confronted Moses for his failure to circumcise his son (Gen. 17:14), which among the Hebrews was to be done eight days after birth. The ritual was also practiced by many of the nations surrounding Israel. However, with other nations, the ritual was more a rite of puberty than the sealing of a divine covenant as it was for Israel.

Circumcision, the physical act of cutting away the foreskin of a male, was one of the most widely practiced Jewish rituals. It was demanded for the descendants of Abraham as the sign of the covenant God had made with Abraham (Gen. 17:9-14). The earliest circumcisions were done with crude instruments like a flint knife. This commandment for circumcision was first given to Abraham (Gen. 17:12) and then reaffirmed to Moses in the wilderness (Lev. 12:3). Although the Law of Moses does not designate who is to perform this surgical procedure on male infants, the common assumption is that an adult male would remove the infant's foreskin. However, on at least one occasion, the wife of Moses, namely, Zipporah, did the circumcision of her son (Exod. 4:25).

Since God's deliverance of the children of Israel from Egyptian bondage was His means to fulfill that covenant and since Moses was designated to represent God in this deliverance, for Moses to ignore this part of the covenant was especially reprehensible. When Zipporah realized that her husband's disobedience had placed his own life in danger, she took matters into her hands and circumcised her son, though in disgust, in order to save her husband's life (Exod. 4:24-26). The incident could well have irreparably damaged the intimacy and fellowship between Moses and Zipporah.

WIFE OF A DIFFICULT MAN

Moses did send his wife with their sons back to her family in Midian (Exod. 18:2-3). No explanation is given as to why or even precisely when they departed. Moses may have feared for their safety during his ongoing confrontations with Pharaoh; Zipporah herself may have decided that the uncertainty of the situation in Egypt was not conducive to rearing children; or the couple may have mutually felt tension developing in their relationship and decided a cooling-off period was needed.

The family was later reunited in the wilderness when the Israelites camped at Mount Horeb after the exodus of the Israelites from Egypt was complete. When his family arrived, Moses seemed more interested in his father-in-law than in his wife and sons. The Bible records an extensive and intimate discussion between the two men, but no interaction between Moses and his wife or children is noted.

Reuel departed for Midian, leaving his daughter and grandsons with Moses. Zipporah then seems to fade from the scene. She probably died and was buried on the way to the Promised Land. In keeping with what seems to be Moses' indifference to his wife, no mention of her death is made in Scripture. Moses later married an Ethiopian woman.

The Bible only reveals bits and pieces of the life of Zipporah. Although her first mention is as a single shepherdess, all that is recorded of her life is connected to Moses. Yet nothing is said in the text about the kind of life Zipporah and Moses had together—their relationship to one another, their intimacy as wife and husband, their family life, their relationship to their children.

PRAYER

Heavenly Father, how challenging to live with a difficult man—one who is pulled in many different ways and who stands under overwhelming pressures or, as Moses, one who carries the burden of a nation and who finds himself reluctantly in the public arena! Give me patience to wait on You and him; give me sensitivity to meet even his unspoken needs.

FURTHER STUDY

ZIPPORAH

- *Name:* Zipporah. (Hb. *tsipporah*, "bird" or "a little bird")
- *Scripture References:* Exodus 2:15-22; 4:20-26; 18:2-6
- *Family:* Daughter of Reuel (Jethro or Hobab), the priest of Midian; one of seven sisters; wife of Moses; mother of Gershom and Eliezer
- *Marital Status:* Married to Moses
- *Occupation:* Shepherdess as a single young woman; homemaker after her marriage to Moses
- *Spiritual Gifts:* None readily apparent
- *Dominant Characteristics:* Decisive, bold, strong-willed, hard-working
- *Dates:* See Miriam's timeline for general time period

EXEGETICAL NOTES

Exodus 2:15 "he sought to kill Moses"

"To kill" (Hb. *harag*) and "killed" are from the same root and suggest the idea of slaying in a general sense—whether justly or unjustly—but most commonly an indication of killing for legal reasons.

Exodus 2:16 "the priest of Midian"

"Midian," a son born to Keturah, the wife of Abraham after Sarah's death (Gen. 25:1-6), produced descendants called Midianites. They were nomads who lived east of the Gulf of Aqabah in the Sinai peninsula. Reuel,"as the priest of Midian," may have had some knowledge of the God of the Hebrews, but the text does not indicate what god he served as priest.

Exodus 2:19 "an Egyptian rescued us"
"Rescued" (Hb. *natsal*) has the sense of plucking out of the hands of an enemy, delivering from oppression, bringing out of trouble and protecting from danger or evil. In fact, there is the hint of a bursting forth from bonds with courage.

Exodus 2:21-22 "Moses agreed to stay"
"Agreed" (Hb. *ya'al*) suggests a willingness, despite difficulty or pain, to undertake challenges.

The name "Gershom" (Hb.), a son of Moses, means "sojourner," coming from the verbal root "drive away" and with the sense of "stranger"—an appropriate name for commemorating Moses' experience as a stranger in a foreign land. Midian was not his home, nor was Egypt (see Gen. 15:13; Exod. 22:21).

PARALLEL REFERENCES

Exodus 4:24-26
And it came to pass on the way [back to Egypt from Midian], at the encampment, that the LORD met him [Moses] and sought to kill him. Then Zipporah took a sharp stone and cut off the foreskin of her son and cast it at Moses' feet, and said, "Surely you are a husband of blood to me!" So He let him go. Then she said, "You are a husband of blood!"— because of the circumcision.

Exodus 18:2-6
Then Jethro, Moses' father-in-law, took Zipporah, Moses' wife, after he had sent her back, with her two sons, of whom the name of one was Gershom (for he said, "I have been a stranger in a foreign land") and the name of the other was Eliezer (for he said, "The God of my father was my help, and delivered me from the sword of Pharaoh"); and Jethro, Moses' father-in-law, came with his sons and his wife to Moses in the wilderness, where he was encamped at the mountain of God. Now he had said to Moses, "I, your father-in-law Jethro, am coming to you with your wife and her two sons with her."

TEACHING OUTLINE

INTRODUCTION

Zipporah is an enigma in the sense that she resisted the divine directive but repented of her defiance and acted decisively to save her husband's life.

I.   The Meeting Happened by Chance (Exod. 2:15-17).
   A. The Place (v. 15)
   B. The Circumstances (vv. 16-17)

II. The Marriage Was Arranged with Purpose (Exod. 2:18-21).
   A. The Daughters' Report (vv. 18-19)
   B. The Father's Reaction (v. 20)
   C. The Decision of Moses and Reuel (v. 21)

III. The Union Produced Offspring (Exod. 2:22).
   A. Son's Birth
   B. The Testimony of His Name

CONCLUSION

The biblical record about Zipporah does not suggest that she is a submissive or loving wife; in fact, she seems detached from Moses. However, when he needed her, she was there to save his life. She also bore two sons for him.

QUOTATIONS

"Like everything which is not the involuntary result of fleeting emotion but the creation of time and will, any marriage, happy or unhappy, is infinitely more interesting than any romance, however passionate." W. H. Auden

"People get from books the idea that if you have married the right person you may expect to go on 'being in love' forever. As a result, when they find they are not, they think this proves they have made a mistake and are entitled to a change—not realizing that, when they have changed, the glamour will presently go out of the new love just as it went out of the old one. In this department of life, as in every other, thrills come at the beginning and do not last.... but if you go through with it, the dying away of the first thrill will be compensated for by a quieter and more lasting kind of interest." C. S. Lewis, *Mere Christianity* (New York: HarperCollins, 1952), 110.

DOROTHY'S DICTUM

God knows the circumstances of life in advance. He expects us to seek His face on our responses to the events of life.

INDUCTIVE QUESTIONS

1. God worked on Moses' character about forty years before sending him back to Egypt at the age of eighty. Zipporah must have been about fifty-five years old or older when she and Moses began the journey to Egypt. Consider how the Lord may have used Zipporah in the decades-long character-building process. Now reflect on what contributions are made by a wife and mother in the personal and spiritual growth of her husband.

2. Although Scripture does not provide details about the personal life shared by Moses and Zipporah, either before or after the exodus, the fact that Moses was reunited with his wife and sons is important enough to be noted specifically (Exod. 18). How does the presence of his wife in the life of a Christian or national leader affect the confidence and trust of the people he leads? Can you think of any contemporary examples?

3. Can you recall circumstances in your own life or that of a woman you know in which decisive action was necessary to protect the spiritual well-being of husband or children?

SCARLET THREAD OF REDEMPTION

Moses again faced death at the hands of the Egyptians. God provided deliverance for him. Moses then offered deliverance to others and continued his journey of faith.

GRIEVING MOTHERS: THE WOMEN WHO HATED HIM

In Egyptian art, women are portrayed prominently as part of the family, which may be a means of recognition for the important contributions made by Egyptian women to society. One of the common designations for elite women on the monuments of Egypt was that of "mistress of the house." This seems to indicate a married woman in charge of conducting the affairs of her household, managing its economy, helping accumulate wealth by exchanging goods they produced, weaving cloth, producing flour and bread, and, of course, bearing and rearing children. Mothers especially were held in great honor.

Whereas most plagues bypassed the Israelites in Goshen, the women of Egypt felt the full brunt of these acts of devastation. Certainly their spiritual world was challenged since the many gods of Egypt were shown to be inadequate. The tranquility of their neighborhoods and communities must have been shattered as they moved from one disaster to another. No relief team or government agency could have responded effectively to so many national crises in such a short time.

Even their most mundane homemaking tasks were repeatedly made more difficult, if not impossible. For example, in the ancient world, women were traditionally the bearers of water, which had to be brought from some distance away. When the water was changed to blood, what was considered the most essential element in survival was contaminated. The women were probably the first to see this crisis arise, and they were the ones to listen to the ranting of their husbands, to calm the fears of their frightened children, and to deal creatively with the crisis created in their domain—i.e., securing pure water for drinking.

The earlier plagues, however, were a peccadillo compared to the final one. Interestingly, both the first plague (the turning of the water, including the Nile River, into blood) and the last plague (the death of the first-born) should have been reminders to the Egyptians of the Hebrew baby boys murdered by royal edict decades before. God did not take lightly the killing of the sons of Israel. The time came for an accounting, and the sons of Egypt were condemned to die.

DEATH OF THE FIRSTBORN

The Egyptian women were hearty, as women have been throughout history. They probably learned quickly how to cope with the escalating crises and how to shepherd the household through the challenges created. But, when the plague struck at their innermost being, i.e., at their maternity—that natural love of a mother for the offspring whom she had carried in her womb, then birthed in the midst of pain and suffering, and with whom she was linked as only a mother can bond with the fruit of her womb—this crisis and this pain went beyond all others. The death of the firstborn could have left a woman without father, husband, brother, and son in one fatal stroke of the death angel.

Surely this fateful and tragic blow must have awakened the women of Egypt to wailing and desperation as never before or since in the nation's history. The losses were overwhelming, and few women before or since could even begin to feel the pain these women felt.

The birth of a child is still a celebratory event. Modern couples may debate questions concerning parenthood that would seem strange in the ancient world: Should you conceive a child? If so, how many children should you bring into the world? When should you begin your family?

In the ancient world, among the Hebrews and even somewhat among their pagan neighbors, the prevalent attitude was that children, as many as come, are wanted now. In fact, the Hebrews considered their children to be a blessing and heritage from the Lord (Ps. 127:3-5). The home was considered the setting for "building" sons and daughters, as described in what has been called "the Builder's Psalm" (Ps. 128).

For many reasons, children, more than money, represented "wealth." The society of the ancient world did more bartering than purchasing. The work to be done was divided among members of the family. Instead of institutions for the sick and aging, children and grandchildren assumed the responsibility of caring for their own elderly family members. Without descendants not only would a couple be bereft of the contributions of children to everyday living, but also an entire family and its legacy would be wiped out (see the story of the widow with two sons in 2 Sam. 14:4-7).

My own firstborn Armour spent a period of six weeks in Uganda during the summer between his sophomore and junior years of high school teaching basketball and performing in exhibition games as part of a mission effort. He had opportunity to get to know the people in the community where he lived and worked. In the Middle East even until now when a son is born, the parents often adopt the name of the son just as the identification of a mother or father is often stated by means of relationship to a son in the Bible. When my husband and I joined Armour for the last few weeks of his assignment, we were introduced to this same custom in an African setting. Immediately, I was recognized as being "Mama Armour" rather than Mrs. Paige Patterson or Dr. Dorothy Patterson! Such a designation not only recognized the unique position of the firstborn son but also acknowledged the importance of children.

These Egyptian women were devastated by the loss of firstborn sons. Perhaps some woman felt that this tragedy wiped out her own identity—a feeling quite normal for a mother who must release her child at any age to the chilling waters of death. Others may have felt a stripping away of life and purpose since the nurturing of children was a high priority and time-consuming task. A mother's bonding with her child usually begins early, runs deep, and stays strong.

Where did these Egyptian women assign the blame? To their ruler? Remember that the Egyptians viewed pharaohs as gods and worshiped them. Most were probably slow to place the responsibility on Pharaoh. On their government? How complacent we become when living seems to be good: The economy strong; the country at peace; life is comfortable.

Although the blame may have been spread around, I am certain that no one received as much as Moses! These women must have hated him with an everlasting hatred. They must have flooded the land with sorrowful wailing over their losses and unleashed angry demands for the immediate departure of Moses. Perhaps they would not dare call for his death, since by this time most would realize that Moses had behind him a supernatural power beyond the gods of Egypt. To call for his death might be the final straw to wipe out the entire population of Egypt; but to be rid of him, never to hear his voice or see his face or to experience the power he seemed to wield—that was their determined and unified cry!

Mothers throughout history have been called upon to give up their sons. It is hard enough when the call is for sons to put their lives on the line in order to protect home and hearth or land of birth and citizenship. The question of what constitutes a just war should not be debated by mothers, or maybe it should! Surely they would handle the lives of their beloved, and often only begotten, sons with more sensitivity and better stewardship than dictators or bureaucrats!

In the minds and hearts of the mothers of Egypt, the devastation of this war against their sons reached beyond what they had considered the protective walls of their dwellings. There had been no call to battle; no cause had been proclaimed or debated; they saw no justice served.

MOTHERS TODAY

Mothers today may unknowingly face a similar battle. This danger is not just the death of the physical body but an assault on the minds and hearts of their sons. When young sons are drawn into pornography by means of television and computer screens found within the home; when they are drawn to commit assault and even murder for the want of some possession, for the anger against some classmate, or for the thrill of participating in violence—and when the seeds for these heinous crimes begin within the walls of home—you know that there is a death angel stalking your own sons and daughters. Such is not justice but exploitation, and that exploitation is at the most vulnerable point! It is a quiet but deadly attack that reaches a child even in what should be the safe boundaries of his home.

Perhaps modern mothers are also lashing out at the wrong targets as they blame the schools their children attend, the neighborhoods in which they live, the friends with whom they play. Mothers should look, not necessarily for deliverance from hardship and suffering that would test their faith but for deliverance unto the faith of their fathers and commitment to the Judeo-Christian foundation found in the Holy Scripture. Such a foundation contributes to the building of a great nation..

When someone lifts a worthy standard, you dare not turn away to take refuge in your comfortable status quo. You dare not be lulled into complacency when a battle rages. You cannot turn your back on what is right for convenience without paying a heavy penalty when wrong prevails. The spiritual lives of your children are at risk.

PRAYER

Lord God, mothers often cry out to you on behalf of their sons. I thank you for those lives entrusted to my care. I ask you for wisdom and strength to give them my best. I ask for willingness to put aside my own personal agenda and allow you to mold their lives. I ask for patience to persevere in the task of mothering.

FURTHER STUDY

EXEGETICAL NOTES

Exodus 12:29 "every firstborn male"
The "firstborn" (Hb. *bekor*) was the one sanctified by devout Israelite parents as required by Mosaic Law (see Exod. 22:29). All "firstborn" males were to be devoted to the Lord because of the events of the first Passover night (Exod. 13:1-2) and not because of any predetermined superiority.

Exodus 12:30 "a loud wailing"
This word (Hb. *tse'aqah*) expresses emotion and fear, i.e., yelling, screaming, a cry of distress.

PARALLEL REFERENCES
Exodus 11:4-6
Then Moses said, "Thus says the LORD: 'About midnight I will go out into the midst of Egypt; and all the firstborn in the land of Egypt shall die, from the firstborn of Pharaoh who sits on his throne, even to the firstborn of the female servant who is behind the handmill, and all the firstborn of the animals. Then there shall be a great cry throughout all the land of Egypt, such as was not like it before, nor shall be like it again.'"

Exodus 12:12
For I will pass through the land of Egypt on that night, and will strike all the firstborn in the land of Egypt, both man and beast; and against all the gods of Egypt I will execute judgment: I am the LORD.

Exodus 13:14-15
So it shall be, when your son asks you in time to come, saying, "What is this?" that you shall say to him, "By strength of hand the LORD brought us out of Egypt, out of the house of bondage. And it came to pass, when Pharaoh was stubborn

about letting us go, that the LORD killed all the firstborn in the land of Egypt, both the firstborn of man and the firstborn of beast. Therefore I sacrifice to the LORD all males that open the womb, but all the firstborn of my sons I redeem."

Numbers 8:17
For all the firstborn among the children of Israel are Mine, both man and beast; on the day that I struck all the firstborn in the land of Egypt I sanctified them to Myself.

Numbers 33:4
For the Egyptians were burying all their firstborn, whom the LORD had killed among them. Also on their gods the LORD had executed judgments.

Psalm 78:51
And destroyed all the firstborn in Egypt,
The first of their strength in the tents of Ham.

Psalm 135:8
He destroyed the firstborn of Egypt,
Both of man and beast.

Psalm 136:10
To him who struck down Egypt in their firstborn,
For His mercy endures forever.

TEACHING OUTLINE
INTRODUCTION
These Egyptian women living during the time of Moses were much like mothers in any generation. They loved their families, and there must have been a unique bonding with the firstborn from their respective wombs. They probably spent their days doing the mundane tasks associated with the running of a household. Certainly a primary function was the nurturing of their children. Perhaps even more than many mothers in this generation will, these women spent long hours with their children.

I.   The Strike of the Lord (Exod. 12:29)
A. Throughout the Land
B. From the House of Pharaoh to the Families of Humble Peasants

II. The Response of the Egyptians (Exod. 12:30)
A. Awakened from Sleep and Life
B. Marked by Weeping and Sorrow in Every Home
C. Overwhelmed by the Lord's Judgment

CONCLUSION

Only those who have lost a child can identify with the overwhelming sorrow that came to these women on that fateful night when the death angel visited the homes of Egypt. Their losses were not confined to children since some had fathers, husbands, or brothers who were also firstborn males.

Few women could begin to feel the pain and sense of loss these women felt as those whom they loved were snatched away one by one! They must have been filled with anger over the seemingly useless loss of life. The emotions of these women were pulled in many different directions, and they did not have the spiritual underpinnings of a bedrock faith in the one true and living God to sustain them.

QUOTATIONS

"Bereavement following the death of a child is more intense than any other form of grief. The pain is like an open sore that fails to heal. Time and time again a temporary scar forms, only to break open again with no warning….Things are never the same. We have come to see that life is temporary and that we have no real control." Catherine M. Sanders, *How to Survive the Loss of a Child: Filling the Emptiness and Rebuilding Your Life* (Roseville, CA: Prima Publishing, 1998), 2.

A group of parents describing their experiences of grief after the loss of a child write: "We were studies in contrast in those early months. We were filled with rage and yet we felt hollow. Our eyes brimmed with tears and yet they were empty. We could scream but speech came rarely, if at all. We were in excruciating pain and yet we were numb . . . . there was no one who could console us. There was no place to feel secure. We tried to crawl inside ourselves, but even that afforded us no place to hide. It was as if our very being died along with that of our children. We were and remain forever changed." Ellen Mitchell, Carol Barkin et al: *Beyond the Tears: Living after Losing a Child*, rev. ed. (New York: St. Martin's Press, 2009), 9.

"I've known grief through death as a Christian and as a non-Christian. I have observed grief through death among other Christians and non-Christians. There is a difference. The non-Christian displays a grief of despair, of hopelessness, and of helplessness—a grief that often hints of bitterness, unfairness, and a "what am I going to do now?" kind of frustration." Zig Ziglar, *Confessions of a Happy Christian* (Gretna, LA: Pelican Publishing Company, Inc., 1978), 171.

"Sorrow makes us all children again – destroys all differences of intellect. The wisest know nothing." Ralph Waldo Emerson

"We understand death for the first time when he puts his hand upon one whom we love." Madame de Staël

DOROTHY'S DICTUM
Death remains in the divine domain and can strike without warning or human reason. Without the Lord's comfort, there is no hope. With the Lord, there is enough to carry you through even the deepest sorrow.

INDUCTIVE QUESTIONS
1. List some of the questions a parent, perhaps particularly a mother, asks when a son dies. To which of these does Scripture (especially the New Testament) provide an answer? Which of them can only God answer?

2. What differences have you observed between the way Christians and non-Christians grieve the death of a loved one?

3. Why were the firstborn sons of the Israelites spared (See Exod. 12:12-13, 21-23)?

4. How was this event analogous to Jesus' death on the cross (see Exod. 13:1-2, 11-15; 1 Cor. 5:7)?

SCARLET THREAD OF REDEMPTION

Redemption is on God's terms. The Israelites who obeyed God were spared from the plague of death on the firstborn; the Egyptians who spurned the Lord were marked by the stench of death within their households (Exod. 12:12-13, 23-30).

RELUCTANT TRAVELERS: THE WOMEN WHO FEARED HIM

The women of Israel were introduced to Moses in Egypt. Their homes were not the object of the plagues since most of these did not enter the area in which the Hebrews lived. Nevertheless, they must have lived in fear of what plague might suddenly invade their homes. They would have been concerned about the danger in which they and their families lived. They had to exist with the realization that Pharaoh could simply annihilate the Hebrews in retaliation for the grief endured by the Egyptians, all because of the plagues Moses introduced.

The exodus from Egypt, though deliverance from slavery, was not all happiness and joy. Surely the Israelite women had fear in their hearts when they saw the Egyptian troops pursuing them. They could have easily forgotten the awesome power of God, which they had already observed, and begun to hate the man whom they held responsible for what looked to be imminent destruction. Perhaps an old Yiddish proverb describes the scene, "A man makes plans and God laughs," or by interpretation: When an individual acts as if she is in control, she becomes oblivious to the fact that God is working behind the scenes to accomplish His own purpose and plan.[1]

Indeed this awesome spectacle was God's show! Destruction did come—to the enemies of God and of His people; deliverance from slavery was complete—

---

[1] Rabbi Joseph Telushkin, *Biblical Literacy* (New York: Wm. Morrow & Co., 1997), 100.

111

for the children of Israel who were led out of Egypt by Moses. The providence of God was never any more evident.

The laborious journey of this unlikely travel group consisting of some 600,000 Israelite men, together with their wives, children, livestock, and what is described as a "mixed multitude," lasted forty years (Exod. 12:38; 16:35; Num. 11:4; 13:3).The route consisted of much backtracking through land marked by just about as many thorns as brushwood. No wind or breeze came to relieve the heat. With about two million people, together with their herds and livestock, only ten to twelve miles could be covered daily. The barren desert was unforgiving and demanded that the day's journey get them to the next source of water (Num. 33). Even though the people had been slaves in Egypt and had experienced oppression and difficulties, they were not prepared for the privation of the barren wilderness. In Egypt they at least had food, shelter, and a measure of order in their lives.

In light of archaeological evidence of treasures of gold and precious gemstones, elegant textiles, exquisitely carved furnishings found in the Egyptian tombs—all of which indicated a colorful and even luxurious life, you are hard put to find much more than what might be described as mundane and monotonous daily life among the people of Israel, especially during their sojourn in Egypt. This austere lifestyle would be a departure from what is found elsewhere in archaeological sites and what is described in the Old Testament as a love of bright colors and the widespread use of cosmetics and jewelry on the part of the Israelites (Exod. 25:4; 2 Sam. 1:24; 13:18; Prov. 31:22).

The euphoria accompanying deliverance from slavery was short-lived. Soon the women had to deal with husbands and children who were thirsty and hungry and grumbling about it (Exod. 16:3)! In their view, God had moved them from one dead-end street to another! In Egypt, their demise as slaves would have been from oppression; in the wilderness, their death would come from starvation. Whereas God seemed far removed from them in Egypt, He appeared to be the executioner stalking them in the desolate wilderness. They had begun to see His deliverance as the door to their destruction.

After I married my childhood sweetheart, we continued our university training in West Texas, only to discover that I had developed serious allergies to flora and fauna native to the area. Instead of pursuing graduate work elsewhere in the state a safe distance from my health's waterloo and yet still in the midst of familiar surroundings near family and friends and assured employment, we followed what we believed to be divine leadership far south to another state. New Orleans, Louisiana, was a long way from Abilene, Texas!

My husband and I had no jobs and no friends, but we anticipated great adventure and even felt the smug assurance that we were extending my protection from the allergies that had pursued me so relentlessly in West Texas. However, within a few months' time the allergies were back with a vengeance, and I had some questions for God!

What was this plague reigning over my life? My husband and I had followed God to the "wilderness" to escape the oppression of a chronic illness—leaving behind a "secure" life in our home state among friends and family! And for what? To face the same scenario of debilitating illness without the support of extended family and with the challenge of finding new doctors did not seem a good solution!

Oh, yes, I learned about the basic sustenance found in the "manna" of God's presence, which was indeed there to carry me through each day. However, there was no real deliverance from that physical bondage until several decades had passed and many life lessons had been learned!

Widespread hunger among the multitude of Israelites could not be alleviated without some ongoing intervention from God. Can you imagine trying to feed a family three meals a day with any one ingredient alone? "Manna" (Hb., literally "What is it?") was God's solution. It fell daily and without fail from the beginning of their wilderness sojourn until they entered the Promised Land and began to eat of the land's bountiful produce. Although no "manna" fell on the Sabbath, the Hebrews received a double portion the day before so that each Israelite had exactly the amount of "manna" needed to sustain life. On the other hand, any excess gathered, other than the double portion on the eve of Sabbath, would spoil overnight and could not be eaten.

Although no "manna" fell on the Sabbath, the Hebrews received a double portion the day before so that each Israelite had exactly the amount of "manna" needed to sustain life. On the other hand, any excess gathered, other than the double portion on the eve of Sabbath, would spoil overnight and could not be eaten.

"Manna" could have been the best tasting delicacy ever to reach the human palate, but what family would be satisfied with the same monotonous menu three meals a day for forty years? The women must have learned to prepare it with as many variations as humanly possible. But even for a creative cook how many variations are possible for "manna"?

The whining on the part of the Hebrews over their monotonous diet quickly overshadowed any gratitude. God did finally send enough meat to satisfy them. He sent them vast numbers of quail, which drowned out their complaints and brought some measure of satisfaction (Num. 11:20).

DID YOU KNOW?

The Bible describes "manna" as being like coriander seed, white in color and with a taste like honey wafers (Exod. 16:31). Some modern-day scientists suggest that "manna" was really supplied by the Tamarix mannifera, *a tree found even now in the Sinai peninsula. The sap that drips from the tamarisk tree is described as "sweet like honey" and as "sticking to the teeth." There are some differences between the "manna" described in the Bible and the fruit of the modern tamarisk. Finding the tamarisk seems to depend on favorable, but unpredictable, winter rains, and thus it is available only during certain seasons of the year; the "manna" was available every day for forty years. The quantity of tamarisk would not begin to feed three to four million people even for one day! The tamarisk fell from twigs on its tree, and the Bible describes "manna" as falling from heaven. The tamarisk could be preserved for lengthy periods, but the "manna" had no shelf life—no matter what preservative was used; it had to be gathered daily. Tamarisk seems very limited in usage; whereas "manna" was boiled or ground and then prepared in different ways with enough nutrients to provide a healthy diet for an entire nation.[2]*

Meal planning was not the only challenge to the women of Israel. Their clothing inventory was meager—essentially what they wore on their backs out of Egypt—and this same clothing was worn from Egypt to Canaan during the forty-year journey. What a bittersweet experience! The good news was that this clothing proved to be the all-time winner for durability since it did not wear out or disintegrate through four decades of wear under conditions not conducive to good garment care. The bad news was that there was not much opportunity for making a fashion statement that had not already been made for forty years!

No information is available on how the clothing adjusted to the "ins and outs" of aging and wear and to the challenges of fluctuating sizing, but the Bible says that the clothes and shoes worn by the Israelites did not wear out (Deut. 29:5). Nevertheless, even if the women themselves adjusted to the monotony of wearing the same garments day after day and year after year, they still had to deal with children and teens who did not have the maturity or spiritual sensitivities to understand their situation or to understand the difference between where they had been and where they were going.

Answering questions about where they were going and when they would arrive was another challenge that probably fell to the mother. Any day excursion can elicit countless questions from restless passengers, and this wilderness trek was done without wheels or air-conditioning, not to mention

---

[2] Werner Keller, *The Bible as History*, trans. William Neil, (New York: Bantam Books, 1982), 122-24.

electronic games, books, or a swimming pool at the end of the day! There must also have been some apprehension on the part of the mothers of Israel as to the safety of their families, and their intuitions were more likely to be swayed by what seemed to be "relative" safety left behind in what they knew in Egypt to launch out into what they did not know in the journey to the Promised Land.

Their memories of Egypt included a dwelling that at least provided shelter from the elements, food—with some variety—that met their dietary needs, clothing that may have been threadbare and lacking in style but that did change over a period of years, and some reasonable idea of what the future would hold. In the wilderness there was no cupboard and the absence of work and basic sustenance.

The further you move from the hurts and difficulties of the past, the more they fade from view. Women know that well. A mother goes through nine tiring and tedious months of bearing a child with all the discomforting challenges entailed; the baby arrives, sometimes after twenty-four to forty-eight hours of hard labor and sometimes accompanied with the pain of major surgery on top of that. Then follow the sleepless nights, tiring demands of meeting the needs of one totally dependent on you. But within a year or two or three, that same mother may be ready and even eager to go down that road again. The joy of nurturing a child and experiencing the child's loving attachment can overshadow even the most overwhelming difficulties of the birthing process through which she has passed in earlier years.

Moses determined early in this journey that it would take time—much more than he had ever imagined—and even some strange detours to blend these refugees and wanderers into a national group who would be willing to make the necessary sacrifices and trials in order to establish a nation. A new generation had to emerge.

PRAYER

Lord God, I seem to be wandering in the wilderness of my own life with the challenges and obstacles I must face en route to the promised rest you will provide on the other side. Strengthen my faith; lead me through the valleys of discouragement; help me climb the mountains of challenge to heights where I can enjoy the blessings that come from obedience to your plan. Let me forget the murmuring for what I don't have and remember to say thanks for all that you have provided.

FURTHER STUDY

EXEGETICAL NOTES

Exodus 16:1 "departed from Elim"

"Elim" was a place with springs and palm trees, ideally suited for rest. The "Wilderness of Sin", in contrast, was a barren desert west of the Sinai plateau. This rocky wasteland could indeed inspire murmuring among the Israelites on their journey.

Exodus 16:2 "grumbled against Moses and Aaron"

"Grumbled" (Hb. *lun*, "murmur") has the sense of showing obstinacy and stubbornness. It comes from a root meaning "pass the night or remain" in the sense of persisting in whining and murmuring. Their complaining was despite the fact that they were seeing a miracle every day!

Exodus 16:3 "died by the LORD's hand"

Death "by the LORD's hand" could have referred to death by natural causes. The people were suggesting that early death might have come regardless of whether or not they had obeyed the Lord. Their lack of confidence in God's faithfulness clouded their perception of the circumstances and distorted their memories of the past oppression in Egypt. In reality, they refused to believe the promises of God.

Exodus 16:4 "gathered enough for that day"

This phrase underscored that yesterday's "manna" would not be good for the present day's need. What a valuable lesson for believers: You must have God's sustenance every day!

Exodus 16:7 "the LORD's glory"

"Glory" (Hb. *kavod*, "being heavy") had the sense of portraying power and wisdom, which would indicate the greatness and honor due. God's provision, which the people would know and see, helped them understand the wonder of the Lord as their deliverer! This testimony should have enabled the people to process the challenges of life and make their decisions accordingly.

Exodus 16:16, 36 "you may take two quarts"
One "omer" is measured as two quarts or 2.272 liters.

Exodus 16:23 "a holy Sabbath"
"Sabbath" (Hb. *shabbath*) suggested a special observance honoring resting from work and calling for a unique focus on the Lord. It was observed on the seventh day of the week to remind the people to reflect on the Lord's covenant with them and to commemorate His completing of creation.

PARALLEL REFERENCES

Deuteronomy 29:1-19

These are the words of the covenant which the LORD commanded Moses to make with the children of Israel in the land of Moab, besides the covenant which He made with them in Horeb.

Now Moses called all Israel and said to them: "You have seen all that the LORD did before your eyes in the land of Egypt, to Pharaoh and to all his servants and to all his land—the great trials which your eyes have seen, the signs, and those great wonders. Yet the LORD has not given you a heart to perceive and eyes to see and ears to hear, to this very day. And I have led you forty years in the wilderness. Your clothes have not worn out on you, and your sandals have not worn out on your feet. You have not eaten bread, nor have you drunk wine or similar drink, that you may know that I am the LORD your God. And when you came to this place, Sihon king of Heshbon and Og king of Bashan came out against us to battle, and we conquered them. We took their land and gave it as an inheritance to the Reubenites, to the Gadites, and to half the tribe of Manasseh. Therefore keep the words of this covenant, and do them, that you may prosper in all that you do.

"All of you stand today before the LORD your God: your leaders and your tribes and your elders and your officers, all the men of Israel, your little ones and your wives—also the stranger who is in your camp, from the one who cuts your wood to the one who draws your water—that you may enter into covenant with the LORD your God, and into His oath, which the LORD your God makes with you today, that He may establish you today as a people for Himself, and that He may be God to you, just as He has spoken to you, and just as He has sworn to your fathers, to Abraham, Isaac, and Jacob.

"I make this covenant and this oath, not with you alone, but with him who stands here with us today before the LORD our God, as well as with him who is not here with us today (for you know that we dwelt in the land of Egypt and that we came through the nations which you passed by, and you saw their abominations and their idols which were among them—wood and stone and silver and gold); so that there may not be among you man or woman or family or tribe, whose heart turns away today from the LORD our God, to go and serve the gods of these nations, and that there may not be among you a root bearing bitterness or wormwood; and so it may not happen, when he hears the words of this curse, that he blesses himself in his heart, saying, 'I shall have peace, even though I follow the dictates of my heart'—as though the drunkard could be included with the sober.

TEACHING OUTLINE

INTRODUCTION

Although one dare not attempt to stereotype all the women of Israel in any generation, you would certainly assume that any woman who made it very far in this grueling journey must have been a woman of strength. These women faced almost insurmountable difficulties. They must have lived under the constant pressure of uncertainty, fearing for their lives and for the lives of their families.

The creativity of these wandering women must have been stretched day by day and even hour by hour as they sought to prepare meals with a single ingredient and maintain a measure of happiness within their households during the monotony of a rigorous journey that stretched into decades! Their faith was challenged as they faced the future without knowing anything about the place to which they journeyed and without maps or prearranged lodging for the lengthy trip.

I.   Review of the Journey (Exod. 16:1-3)
     A. The Challenging Route (v. 1)
     B. The Weary Travelers (v. 2)
     C. The Prevailing Attitude (v. 3)

II. The Itinerary (Exod. 16:4-31)
     A. The Menu of Provision (vv. 4-6)
     B. The Response of Whining (vv. 7-16)
     C. The Lord's Judgment (vv. 17-21)
     D. The Gift of the Sabbath (vv. 22-31)

III. The Destination (vv. 35-36)

CONCLUSION

Many women today face similar uncertainties. Unemployment, medical emergencies, natural disasters. Countless other difficulties arise to challenge their peaceful existence and drive them to the wilderness of doubt and fear.

The women of Israel complained and even on occasion rebelled against the leader whom God had placed over them. However, most of them were survivors who plodded along, vacillating between exhilarating faith and bitter discouragement. Some must have risen to the top with an unshaken faith and consistent hope.

QUOTATIONS

"Yes, I suppose I am as happy in my dear, precious husband and children as a wife and mother can be in a fallen world, which must not be a real heaven lest we should love the land we journey through so well as to want to pitch our tents in it forever, and cease to look and long for the home whither we are bound." Elizabeth Prentiss, *Stepping Heavenward* (New York: Anson D. F. Randolph & Company, 1880), 295.

"I have learned that in every circumstance that comes my way, I can choose to respond in one of two ways: I can whine—or—I can worship!" Nancy Leigh deMoss, *Choosing Gratitude: Your Journey to Joy* (Chicago: Moody Publishers, 2009), 23.

"I'd much rather be known as kind, joyful, grateful, and encouraging, rather than grumbling, whiny, discouraging, and complaining . . . . What comes out of our mouths paints a picture of what is in our hearts. If we are growing in our trust in the Lord, it comes out in our words of hope and contentment no matter what the circumstances. Yet if people hear bitterness, gossip, and frustration pour out of our mouths, we reveal the anger and worry in our hearts." Karol Ladd, *Thrive, Don't Simply Survive: Passionately Live the Life You Didn't Plan* (New York: Howard Books, 2009), 133.

DOROTHY'S DICTUM

A wife and mother determines the attitude in her home—desperation because of circumstances or joy in the LORD because of His wonderful providence!

INDUCTIVE QUESTIONS

1. What purpose may God have for allowing your pursuit of His will to be accompanied by frustrations and difficulties?

2. What does complaining reveal about your understanding of God's character and your faith in Him?

3. Why is refraining from voicing within a group your negative assessments of a situation important?

4. What regularly performed tasks of wives and mothers are often taken for granted by their families? How can you brighten the day of a woman who seems discouraged about or weary in doing the mundane but necessary chores of life?

5. Brainstorm ways to nurture an attitude of contentment and gratitude in your life and/or in the lives of your children. Set a goal of putting one of those ideas into action for at least two weeks and journal or discuss your perceptions of improvements made.

SCARLET THREAD OF REDEMPTION

Deliverance is ultimately God's work. He determines the journey. He sends the sustenance through His providence. Finally, He will bring you to the promised rest.

THE ETHIOPIAN: THE OTHER WOMAN HE MARRIED

When Moses entered this biracial marriage, he and his Ethiopian wife experienced instant resistance and even rejection, beginning with his own family. This woman is not named in Scripture or in any other record of the period. She probably loved Moses and he, her; but they both faced bitter hatred and relentless animosity from Moses' family. Nevertheless, some have suggested that she may have been a better companion to Moses than Zipporah!

The Bible has only a passing mention of this Cushite woman, who must have been dark-skinned and perhaps younger and more attractive than Moses' sister Miriam. Her ethnic background linked her to the African country south of the Nile cataracts. Many scholars believe that Ethiopia was too far removed from Moses' sphere of activity. They would suggest that this woman was a member of the people of Cushan, who were neighbors of Midian (see Hab. 3:7).

This Cushite woman could be another reference to Zipporah, the Midianite. That Miriam would wait so long to chastise her brother for a marriage he contracted long before God called him to leadership is highly unlikely even though Miriam might have called Zipporah a Cushite—either because Zipporah herself was from this general region or because she wanted to refer to Zipporah in a contemptuous manner. On the other hand, if Moses had recently married again, probably after Zipporah's death, and had chosen a Cushite woman to be his wife, Miriam could have felt that such a union was a danger to Israel. Even in this case, she was ignoring the fact that God had merely forbidden the Israelites to marry the daughters of Canaan (Exod. 34:16), which would mean that union with a Cushite woman, who either came from the Cushites dwelling in Arabia or from the group of foreigners who had come with the Israelites out of Egypt, would not be expressly forbidden.

Women among the Hebrews enjoyed far more honor and deference than did women of the surrounding pagan nations. Despite the cultural setting in which women were often considered inferior to men, the Hebrew women were responsible for managing their households and nurturing their children. These tasks alone brought them respect and influence. The family has always been the basic unit in Hebrew society.

For the Cushite woman to enter a union with Israel's greatest leader presented simultaneously responsibility and opportunity. Once the commitment to marriage had been made between Moses and the Cushite woman, the Hebrews had the responsibility to accept Moses' wife as one of their own and treat her with the same honor that would be due their own wives and daughters. The Cushite woman had the opportunity to enjoy the honor due Hebrew women in general and to serve the nation alongside her husband.

You can hope that the union of Moses and the Cushite was marked by deep and true love and respectful deference of one for the other. You can wonder if her influence over Moses was strong and positive. You can also speculate as to whether by this time Moses had learned to be more attentive to the needs of his wife than he had been in what was surmised from the sketchy biblical account of his marriage to Zipporah.

Although the Bible does not give much information about the Ethiopian woman Moses married, you can ask questions about her. What were her thoughts about Miriam's attack on Moses? Did she rejoice in the judgment against Miriam? Was she glad to see her sister-in-law banished from the camp?

Answers to these questions would help us to know just what kind of woman Moses married. In the final scene of this drama, the Cushite woman should have been able to identify with Miriam, who because of her sin had become an outcast, a rejected woman. If the Cushite grieved over Miriam's sin and punishment, if her focus was more on the tragedy that afflicted her sister-in-law than upon her own hurt, then you would know that Moses had married a woman with spiritual sensitivities. Perhaps the Cushite woman even interceded for Miriam; perhaps she purchased the two birds required for Miriam's cleansing; perhaps she was waiting for Miriam to return with a place of refuge prepared and forgiveness in her heart for the one who had wronged her and her husband.

Unfortunately, you do not find answers to these questions in the text. However, the questions raised serve as a prick to awaken your own consciousness to issues with which believing women must grapple in their own lives. The Bible does speak on the character required of one who bears the name of Christ!

PRAYER

Heavenly Father, I must contemplate what it means to be an outcast, to be on the outside looking in. Let me be careful to remain on the inside of your divine will. Let me reach out to the unloved and unredeemed and draw them to you. Remove my prejudices and fill me with your unconditional love. Then I can become your channel for blessing.

FURTHER STUDY

FACTS ON MOSES' ETHIOPIAN WIFE

- *Scripture References:* Numbers 12:1
- *Family:* Cushite or Ethiopian heritage
- *Marital Status:* Wife of Moses
- *Occupation:* Homemaker
- *Dates:* She was certainly much younger than Moses and probably did not come into his life until around 1415 BC during his senior years.

EXEGETICAL NOTES

Numbers 12:3 "Moses was a very humble man"
"Humble" (Hb. *'anav*) suggests one who is lowly and meek and who bows because of personal piety. Truly "humble" people like Moses are modest, not lacking confidence but devoid of arrogance and pride; spiritually, they are teachable (Ps. 25:9). This quality underscores that Moses did not flaunt the leadership role assigned to him by God.

Numbers 12:6 "Listen to what I say"
"Hear" (Hb. *shama'*) as an imperative has the force of a command, not merely receiving information but listening or attending to what is said with the intent to obey. In verse 2, the Lord had "heard" or given His attention to the complaint of Miriam and Aaron.

Numbers 12:6, 8 "in a vision"
"Vision" (Hb. *mar'ah*) refers to an apparition. The Lord in some way revealed or manifested Himself visually to one who was "a prophet among you." Miriam, identified as "a prophetess" (Exod. 15:20), may have experienced such a "vision." This mode of revelation is distinguished from God's speaking with Moses "face to face" (Hb. *peh 'el-peh*, lit.

"mouth to mouth"), obviously directly and openly. Unlike "a prophet," who hears from God "in a vision," Moses saw "the form of the LORD" (see 12:8 below).

The Lord also explained that He spoke to such "a prophet" "in a dream" (Hb. *chalom*) as distinguished from the way He spoke with Moses—"plainly, and not in dark sayings" (Hb. *chidah*), i.e., perplexing questions or enigmas. Examples of people to whom God spoke in a dream include Abimelech (Gen. 20:2-6), Jacob (Gen. 31:10-13), Laban (Gen. 31:24), Joseph (Gen. 37:5-10; 42:9), the pharaoh Joseph served (Gen. 41:1-33), as well as the pharaoh's butler and baker (Gen. 40:5-22).

Numbers 12:7 "he is faithful"

"Faithful" (Hb. *'aman*) suggests one who is absolutely reliable and trustworthy. In Hebrew the word is a verb in a participle form, which gives the sense of someone on whom others could lean consistently and therefore highlights Moses' character. One could reasonably expect him to be upright, to follow and deliver the Lord's instructions day in and day out without fail.

Numbers 12:8 "he sees the form of the LORD"

"Form" (Hb. *temunah*) suggests a visible figure or likeness. Moses later warned the Israelites against making carved images "in the form of any figure" (i.e., as idols to worship), explaining that when the Lord spoke to them at Mount Sinai they "heard the sound of the words, but saw no form"; they "only heard a voice" (Deut. 4:12, 15-16, 23). Whatever "form" or manifestation of Himself the Lord allowed Moses to see was apparently not entrusted to anyone else at that time.

PARALLEL REFERENCES
Exodus 33:9-11
And it came to pass, when Moses entered the tabernacle, that the pillar of cloud descended and stood at the door of the tabernacle, and the LORD talked with Moses. All the people saw the pillar of cloud standing at the tabernacle door, and

all the people rose and worshiped, each man in his tent door. So the Lᴏʀᴅ spoke to Moses face to face, as a man speaks to his friend. And he would return to the camp, but his servant Joshua the son of Nun, a young man, did not depart from the tabernacle.

Exodus 34:29-30

Now it was so, when Moses came down from Mount Sinai (and the two tablets of the Testimony were in Moses' hand when he came down from the mountain), that Moses did not know that the skin of his face shone while he talked with Him. So when Aaron and all the children of Israel saw Moses, behold, the skin of his face shone, and they were afraid to come near him.

TEACHING OUTLINE

INTRODUCTION

Buried within the text of Scripture are occasional bits and pieces that challenge your mind and touch your heart. To discover these fragments and piece them together is an intellectual challenge. To contemplate what is not there, i.e., those gaps in the story, is an exercise that does not produce additional facts but nevertheless enables you to put yourself into the life of the shadowy figure and often learn some valuable lessons.

I. The Framework of Opposition—Within the Family (Num. 12:1)
   A. Who—Miriam and Aaron
   B. Against Whom—Moses

II. The Foundation for Opposition (Num. 12:1-2)
   A. Prejudice toward the Wife Moses Chose (v. 1)
   B. Resentment over the Authority of Moses (v. 2)

III. The Lord's Response to Rebellion (Num. 12:4-9)
   A. Direct Confrontation (vv. 4-5)
   B. Plain Words of Rebuke (vv. 6-9)

CONCLUSION

This obscure woman became the wife of one of the most prominent leaders of Israel. Whether a help or a hindrance, she seemingly conducted herself graciously and without bitterness towards her antagonists.

QUOTATIONS

"Ultimately it is God who calls two people together—not diversity of culture or a common missionary spirit." Steve and Mary Prokopchak, *Called Together* (Shippensburg, PA: Destiny Image, 2009), 178.

In his essay for the *Criswell Theological Review* (vol. 6, no. 2 [Spring 2009]) entitled "A Biblical Perspective on Interracial Marriage," J. Daniel Hays thoroughly documents and examines evidence pertinent to both of Moses' marriages. He concludes: "So what theological conclusions should we draw? I would suggest that interracial intermarriage is strongly affirmed by Scripture. Marrying unbelievers, on the other hand, is strongly prohibited. The criteria for approving or disapproving of our children's selected spouses should be based on their faith in Christ and not at all on the color of their skin....

"Furthermore, the common cultural ban on intermarriage lies at the heart of the racial division in the church. White Christians who say that they are not prejudiced but who vehemently oppose interracial marriages are not being honest. They are still prejudiced, and I would suggest that they are out of line with the biblical teaching on this subject. In addition, this theology applies not only to black/white interracial marriages, but equally to intermarriages between any two ethnic groups within the church throughout the world, especially in those regions where the church has inherited strong interracial animosities from the culture at large" (22-23).

DOROTHY'S DICTUM

Jealousy is a poisonous root that breaks family bonds, destroys friendships, and separates one from intimate fellowship with the heavenly Father.

INDUCTIVE QUESTIONS

1. How would your church respond if the wife of your pastor died and he later married a woman of another ethnicity?

2. Pray that the Holy Spirit would make you aware of critical attitudes or stereotypes that are rooted in racial prejudice. Confess these to the Lord and ask Him to replace the prejudice with unbiased and unconditional love for all people.

SCARLET THREAD OF REDEMPTION

The need for forgiveness among sinful women and men—whatever their ethnic background—never ceases, which is why everyone needs a Savior!

Conclusion

Heroes have virtually disappeared from the modern stage of history. Where are the men and women of character who, even when troubled, are still triumphant over the challenges they face? Moses was such a man. He lived with a clear conscience and open life. He was accessible and human, but he was also set apart and in touch with the God of the universe. His life was not a façade of "saintliness" but rather a reflection of selflessness, a lifestyle marked by a standard formulated from biblical absolutes. Moses was never out of touch with the trials and testings of life, but he remained in touch with the God who was able to carry him through such challenges. The women in his life must have been touched by the shadow of his greatness. In fact, there is good reason to believe that these women magnified that shadow by their own exemplary character and heroic actions.

By definition, a hero or heroine is distinguished by courage or ability and admired for brave deeds and noble qualities. For centuries local heroes have been immortalized in statuary found in town squares and city parks, but seemingly the modern trend is to replace the heroes with grotesque abstract sculptures—perhaps because of the paucity of heroes! Heroes who deliver from the enemy or emulate servanthood and selflessness seem to have faded into history. Replacing them are high profile athletes or movie stars who put their influence on the auction block to sell everything from bonnets to bonds. The gulf has continued to widen between what you see as a role model and what you need as a pattern for achievement. Even the furniture you now buy is more likely to be a reproduction rather than a piece fashioned from genuine, solid wood.

HOW TO CRAFT A HERO
Heroes are created by the media and placed before the public like food on the cafeteria line or products on the supermarket shelf; they can be stripped down to the bone and removed from their pedestals by the same people who put them there.

The modern culture is rapidly becoming a society without character. The next generation is being taught to cut corners and accommodate themselves to the lower standards that have already overwhelmed this generation. The shift in values is just like the proverbial camel that started into its master's tent with its nose and soon took over the tent by pushing the master outside! With no common standard or absolutes, heroism simply becomes the preference of one person above another. If you cannot judge that some actions are better than others, you cannot create or select exemplary heroes. Virtue and duty, learning to discern between good and evil, choosing right over wrong should be much more important than fame and fortune, going along to get along, tolerance and compromise.

The trend is to replace heroes with selected "role models," which by very definition should raise a question. Webster defines a "role model" as one whose behavior in some particular role is to be imitated by others. In other words, there are not always the necessary ethical boundaries or absolute characteristics in this value-free definition; a role model can be good or bad. Role models tend to be too much linked to monetary power and professional success. All role models are not created equal, nor should all be automatically welcomed to the list of heroes!

Noble character and courageous actions are another matter, especially when defined with history unmarred by revisionism and with language uncontaminated by distortion. Genuine heroes are going to be marked by behavior and lifestyles encompassing standards far broader than isolated role modeling found only in some specific area of life.

Though the essence of heroism may be extraordinary achievement that seems larger than life, achievements in themselves do not make the hero. For there is nothing heroic in merely doing exceedingly well what you are paid to do. Heroism is also marked by courage. The hero is not as concerned with seeking personal happiness as with working toward corporate goodness, and his satisfaction seems to be found in losing himself by doing good to others (Matt. 16:24-25).

ISRAEL'S GREATEST LEADER

When my husband and I attended an elegant dinner honoring an esteemed North Carolina senator, the occasion was made even more memorable by the presence of a man whose professional persona has impacted several generations. I remembered Charlton Heston as the actor who portrayed Judah Ben-Hur in the multi-Oscar winning, powerful saga of two childhood friends, a Jew and a Roman, who became bitter enemies during the time of Christ. But on this particular evening, my mind was more tuned to Heston's larger-than-life portrayal of Moses. Though now in his eighties and marked by the passing of years, Heston still carried a moral ascendancy and confident demeanor, bringing a hushed awe over the platform as he arose to make his speech. The speech was pertinent and well delivered, but it paled considerably in the wake of the eloquent soliloquy from the final days of Moses, which Heston used to close his presentation.

Moses came to Mount Nebo only to look into the Promised Land, having lost his opportunity to enter its borders. The greatest leader Israel had ever known and a man distinguished in the annals of world leaders was buried by God Himself in an unmarked grave. A hush fell over the room as we entered a living drama, caught up in the emotions of both men—Moses who lived through the events and Heston who relived them for us.

Few people are willing to put it all on the line for principle, even to pay the ultimate price of laying down a life. Heston himself has stood tall for the importance of character and has maintained a personal commitment to the Judeo-Christian ethic all through the years, even while working in the midst of an environment where he was in the minority. Heston was a God-fearing man who honored his Creator in life and work; he was a one-woman man and a doting father; he served his country well and remained an outspoken patriot as long as he lived; he gave his fans a genuine hero who exemplified the greatness of character portrayed on the silver screen throughout the warp and woof of his own lifestyle.

But Moses—he is another man. Even Heston himself would probably feel inadequate in the presence of this towering giant. The spirit of Moses—perhaps more than anything else his belief in something far greater than himself—sets him apart. Most would have given up, even turned and run, before the challenges Moses faced. In the words of William Wallace (the hero of Scotland as portrayed in the movie *Braveheart*) as he delivered a stirring challenge to Robert the Bruce, the nobleman destined to become Scotland's first real king: "What does that mean—to be noble? Your title gives you claim to the throne of our country, but men don't follow titles, they follow courage! Just lead them to freedom, and they'd follow you."[1]

What separated Moses from his peers? What made him a deliverer who is still remembered as a hero? What about him intrigued the women in his life? What awakened in them the courage and devotion to risk their lives and give up personal pursuits to pour themselves into the life and work of Moses? Was it simply Moses' fame in delivering the Israelites from their Egyptian oppressors and to the borders of the Promised Land? Was it the notoriety and publicity he achieved because of his confrontations with Pharaoh and the plagues he predicted and called forth on the Egyptians? What has given him staying power in remaining a hero in the eyes of Jews and Gentiles alike? Was it the movies about his life, the books about his deeds (especially the Holy Bible)? Was

---

[1] Randall Wallace, *Braveheart*, 86 [online]; accessed 22 November 2010; available from http://www.screenplay.com/downloads/scripts/Bravheart.pdf; Internet.

it the charisma he effused with his presence or his ability as a wordsmith—this man who wanted to depend on his brother Aaron to do his talking because of his own shyness and paucity of words?

None of the above is really essential in making a hero. Rather the heart of the makeover of an ordinary person into an extraordinary leader seems to be found in an unfailing and determined commitment to principle and integrity. Knowledge, wisdom, discernment, compassionate interest in others, an opportunity to enter the stage of history in a dramatic way—these may come into play in varying degrees. Charlton Heston described his hero Moses as an angry man, but a man of courage and faith; an humble and shy man whose inner resources helped him articulate the message God gave him to deliver and to move forward with boldness in the mission he had been given by God Himself.

To understand the making of Moses the hero, you must strip away the outer veneer and reach into the heart and soul of the individual to find the motivating force at the core of his life. There you will find the inner resources of character and the outer manifestations of talents and giftedness that enable an ordinary man or woman to become extraordinary.

THE WOMEN IN HIS SHADOW

However, I want you to look beyond Moses, the readily recognized hero, to the women who stood with him, though often in his shadow—women who risked their lives for him, who selflessly gave themselves for him, and who loved and honored him despite his seeming lack of sensitivity to them. Since much human behavior results from our efforts to emulate others, let's reach up and out to these women of history and seek to uncover the character traits that placed them in the line of fire—a fire that would fashion a pure and most valuable metal of character. Such character must surely be marked by godliness, selflessness, and courage, as well as with extraordinary accountability for the use of personal giftedness and opportunity!

A COLLAGE OF HEROINES

Who will be your heroines? Corrie ten Boom forgave her Nazi tormentors and presented the gospel to them. Ruth Graham reared and nurtured her children in the Lord and honored her husband, even though the famous evangelist was often absent from home traveling throughout the world on kingdom business. Elisabeth Elliot exhibited supreme selflessness in forgiving the murderers of her husband and even leading them to Christ.

Or will you go back to Scripture to lift up exemplary women? Esther submitted herself first to her foster parent, then to the pagan ruler who was also her husband, and ultimately to God. She even put her life on the line in order to save her people. Ruth, though bereft of husband and separated from her birth family and homeland, selflessly sought to meet the needs of her bitter mother-in-law in a foreign land. Mary, the mother of the Messiah, so yielded her life and womb to the Father that she put her reputation and even her life on the line to become the mother of Jesus. Sarah honored her husband Abraham even when he seemed to abandon her to the dangers of a pagan harem.

My list of heroines would be a collage including women from the Bible, women in history, and women whom I have personally known and loved. I admire Esther and learn from her the rewards of submission; I adore Ruth and see in her the joy of a servant's heart; I am fascinated by Abigail and the creativity she used to save her household and win the heart of a king; I am inspired by Hannah whose maternity added a unique dimension to her kingdom service; I am wowed by the "woman of strength" in Proverbs, who becomes a paradigm for all who would be wives and mothers; I reach out and touch Priscilla as I seek to imitate the partnership she had with her husband in life and work; I am a kindred spirit with both Martha and Mary since I love the duties associated with managing a household and extending hospitality, while not wanting to give up sitting at the feet of the Master and learning from Him.

From the pages of history I remember Katie Luther for her management of a complex household interwoven with ministries; I view Susanna Spurgeon and her unique partnership with her pastor/husband in his worldwide ministry as a wonderful model; I learn from Susannah Wesley the sacrifices and rewards of maternity; I am reminded by Sarah Edwards of the challenges of living with a difficult man devoted to serving Christ.

In my own small world, I remember Sarah Eddleman who taught me many things about being the "First Lady" on a seminary campus; I am still inspired by women like Elisabeth Elliot and Jill Briscoe who open the Bible to women and incorporate its principles into their own lives as wives and mothers; I learned the art of gracious hospitality from Ruth Hunt whose open heart and home generously dispensed loving kindness; I have had living lessons in mothering and grandmothering from my own godly mother, Doris Kelley, who lovingly nurtured me and helped me pass on to my children and grandchildren a godly heritage.

What's the point? What can I add to my collage of heroines by studying these women whose lives were intertwined with Moses? As a mother, I have walked through the valley of the shadow of death physically, emotionally, and spiritually with my son just as did Jochebed with Moses—beginning with the trauma at birth and extending to subsequent years of rearing him to adulthood. Although not a health professional, I met the issue of sanctity of life head-on with what seemed to be an untimely pregnancy, and many in this generation struggle with choices of abortion and infanticide as did the midwives who delivered Moses. As the sister of a prominent man, I have invested myself in my brother's life in a myriad of ways. I understand Miriam's maternal ties to her youngest brother. On the other hand, I, too, like the daughter of Pharaoh, was an adoptive mother who faced a heart-wrenching struggle to bond with a child (actually a teenager when she entered my life) from another woman's womb, and I experienced the anxieties and frustration of overcoming natural maternal ties in order to rear a child God sent to my doorstep. As a wife, I, as Zipporah, want the primary devotion of my husband—his provision, protection, leadership, and tender affection—not just qualitatively but also quantitatively!

SISTERS IN OUR CHALLENGES

What women would not rise up with raging anger and overwhelming grief over the untimely death of their sons, husbands, fathers, brothers? What women would not cry out in bitter frustration on a forty-year trip without transportation or maps and with "no-star" food and lodging! What innocent woman would not lose heart in trying to enter her husband's powerful and famous family only to meet animosity and rejection?

Yes, the women in the life of Moses are just like you and me. They experienced the same emotions, similar frustrations, comparable challenges, and, as we, had to do it all living with, or at least in the wake of, a difficult man! From their lives, we can learn what to do and what not to do. We can embrace a faith like that of Jochebed; we do well to imitate the courage of Puah and Shiphrah; we can admire the resourcefulness of Miriam; we are moved by the compassions of Pharaoh's daughter; we are a bit intimidated by the boldness of Zipporah; we are not surprised by the love the Egyptian women had for their firstborn sons; we are impressed with the ingenuity of the women of Israel in clothing and feeding a family for forty years without so much as a retail outlet or grocery store; we are intrigued by a young wife who would accept the challenge of caring for an aging patriarch in the midst of hostility from his family and followers.

For better or worse, we as women will all be related to some man. Oh, he likely will not have the fame or notoriety of Moses. But, he will present some of the same challenges. There will be calls to selflessness as in the life of Jochebed, courage as exemplified in Puah and Shiphrah, creativity and resourcefulness as modeled by Miriam, compassion as seen in Pharaoh's daughter, boldness as found in Zipporah, sorrow as that which poured from the hearts of the Egyptian mothers, perseverance as observed in the women of Israel, mistreatment as experienced by the Cushite woman. In a sense, we are all sisters in our challenges, joys, and pain.

PRAYER

Lord, let me be like Jochebed, willing to risk and spend my life to nurture my children in the years they are entrusted to me but also releasing them at the divinely appointed time. Let me have the courage of Puah and Shiphrah to protect life, especially the most innocent and fragile life among us.

Let me willingly offer to you my creativity and resourcefulness. As Miriam, let me give to them of my time and energy. Keep me free from jealousy and give me quiet joy in working "behind the scenes."

Let my mercies and compassions flow out even to those who have a different ethnic heritage or who do not share my faith commitment. Let my maternity stretch beyond my own family even as did the daughter of Pharaoh.

Let me be sensitive, like Zipporah, to occasions for boldness and times for action. Yet let me also maintain a loving respect for my husband even when I do not understand his actions.

If the cup of sorrow that overwhelmed my Egyptian sisters passes to me through the loss of a loved one, I pray for the comforting presence of the "God of all comfort," whose grace is sufficient even for such overwhelming tragedy. As the cup passes to other women in my circle of friends, I pray for sensitivity and gentleness to reach out to one who is hurting.

Let me meet the challenges and adversities in my life with perseverance just as the women of Israel rose to face their trials and difficulties. Let me set a tone of joyful faith, believing the providences of God are sufficient.

Let me respond to prejudice and injustice in a gracious way as the Cushite woman seemed to do. Keep me free from bitterness and anger and help me to leave judgment in your hands. Lord, take my life and let it be a beautiful, divinely fashioned mosaic!

ROTHY KELLEY PATTERSON

BOOKS IN PRINT

A Woman Seeking God: Discover God in the Places of Your Life
Broadman, 1992 ISBN: 0-8054-5351-2

BeAttitudes for Women: Wisdom from Heaven for Life on Earth.
Wipf and Stock, 2008 (reprint) ISBN: 1-6060-8012-1

The Family: Unchanging Principles for Changing Times
Broadman, 2001 ISBN: 0-8054-2151-3

A Handbook for Minister's Wives
Broadman and Holman, 2002 ISBN: 978-0-8054-2063-0

A Handbook for Parents in Ministry
Broadman and Holman, 2004. ISBN: 0-8054-2786-4

EDITORSHIPS (volumes in print)

The Woman's Study Bible
Thomas Nelson, 2006 (2nd ed.) ISBN: 0-7180-1817-6

Women's Evangelical Commentary on the New Testament
Broadman and Holman, 2006. ISBN: 0-8054-2855-0 or
0-8054-9567-3

FORTHCOMING

Women's Evangelical Commentary on the Old Testament
Broadman and Holman, 2011. ISBN: 0-8054-2856-9

FEMININE THREADS

*Women in the
Tapestry of
Church History*

Diana Lynn Severance

From commoner to queen, the women in this book embraced the freedom and the power of the Gospel in making their unique contributions to the unfolding of history. Wherever possible, the women here speak for themselves, from their letters, diaries or published works. The true story of women in Christian history inspires, challenges and demonstrates the grace of God producing much fruit throughout time.

"I recommend every woman read and study this and keep it within reach for reference and inspiration!"

DOROTHY KELLEY PATTERSON,
Southwestern Baptist Theological Seminary, Fort Worth, Texas

"Well researched and well written, this study of "feminine threads" in Christian history makes for a tapestry of inspiration and instruction for all who love the Lord and his church - men and women alike."

TIMOTHY GEORGE,
Beeson Divinity School, Samford University, Birmingham, Alabama

"...with lively prose and scholarly care she has given us an excellent overview of the various ways in which Christian women have sought to live for Christ."

MICHAEL A. G. HAYKIN,
The Southern Baptist Theological Seminary, Louisville, Kentucky

ISBN 978-1-84550-640-7